# Lessons I Learned from My Mother

# Lessons I Learned from My Mother

## A Reflection on the Past, a Critique of the Present, and Guidance for the Future

### DR. MICHAEL L. SANSEVIRO

iUniverse, Inc.
Bloomington

# LESSONS I LEARNED FROM MY MOTHER
## A Reflection On The Past, A Critique Of The Present, And Guidance For The Future

iUniverse books may be ordered through booksellers or by contacting:

iUniverse
1663 Liberty Drive
Bloomington, IN 47403
www.iuniverse.com
1-800-Authors (1-800-288-4677)

ISBN: 978-1-4620-6872-2 (sc)
ISBN: 978-1-4620-6874-6 (hc)
ISBN: 978-1-4620-6873-9 (ebk)

Printed in the United States of America

iUniverse rev. date: 11/29/2011

# DEDICATION

To My Mother: For making the tough choices that gave me a solid foundation upon which to grow, fail, learn, and succeed.

To Kyle: For your years of patience and support, and always being there while I was busy doing the things I needed and wanted to do to create this successful life.

# PREFACE

Life is full of lessons, some borne of pleasure and some of pain. Sometimes, the lessons we must learn inflict pain (or ideally pleasure) upon others. The learning process can be simple or very complex, bearing instant enlightenment and/or gratification, or knowledge so subtle that the pupil (or teacher) remains unaware of the lessons for the better part of a lifetime. The latter are the lessons that most intrigue me, and upon which I frequently reflect when I think about my mother. Each chapter of this book reflects on a thematic lesson that I learned, and a few anecdotal memories from growing up through which I learned these lessons. I've asked my mother and other selected friends and relatives to read these stories and provide me with feedback, from which other stories or themes may have emerged. To keep this work brief and accessible, I've selected some memories from my point of view that best reflect what I think my mother was trying to teach me.

My mother never believed in "beating a dead horse," so I will try to refrain from doing so herein. These stories from my past have brought laughter and tears, not just to those who lived them but those who have lived through the continual retelling at various gatherings of family and friends throughout the years. My intention is two-fold: both to share a very personal memoir of my mother, but also to reflect from my current professional vantage point lessons that others might find helpful when engaging with their own children.

My mother also believed in giving credit where credit is due. Since the remainder of this book focuses on the intentional and unintentional lessons acquired from my mother, I want to briefly acknowledge a few lessons gleaned from others. Many influential people in my life have taught me critical lessons that are deeply ingrained in my character. None of this is rocket science, and people may read through this book and think, "I could have written this. This is pretty much common sense." Maybe, but I've learned that common sense isn't so common anymore, and at the end of the day anyone could have done anything. It is who actually did it that matters.

First, I reflect on my father. As far back as I can remember, my father would say "your name is all you have." Everything you do determines what that name is worth. Every time you are about to do something, think about how it will impact your name, i.e., your reputation. My father would harp on about how he worked hard to make something of our family name and it was my responsibility to not mess it up. As a kid I read this to mean "don't embarrass me." My father tended to be a "glass half empty" more so than a "glass half full" type of guy, so his focus was more on not screwing up, but I got the positive subtly of the message. Make something of yourself, adding value to your name, so you have something untarnished to pass on to your children. Minimally each generation is expected to achieve at least what the generation before did, but really a bit more is expected. I hope I have cared well for this name that was given me, and I hope my younger siblings come to learn this lesson sooner rather than later. Seeing what generations before me and now basically a generation after me are doing with this name—my name—has reinforced the years of hard work that go into building a name and the fleeting errors in judgment that can destroy it.

Second, I reflect on my grandfather (my mother's father). He was born on a small Caribbean island called Saba, and came to New York City in difficult times with hopes and dreams for himself and his family. My grandfather was one of the hardest working people I've even known. Good was never good enough, especially if you knew you could do better. There was no such thing as punching a time clock in his world—you worked whenever there was work to be done, even if it wasn't your own work. As long as someone needed your help, you had a moral obligation to help, even when that person might not realize they need your help. With this great strength of character and work-ethic came some faults. My grandfather wasn't always one to think through every angle of a situation or contemplate the unintended impact on those he was helping, or those who may have had to sacrifice so the perceived needy could receive his assistance. For example, one day I came home from school and my bicycle was missing. I asked him what happened to it, and he said he shipped it off to Aruba for my cousin because he needed a bicycle.

"But it was my bicycle," I protested.

"You weren't really using it anymore, and your cousin needs it more than you do," was his response.

End of discussion. When my grandfather was done discussing something, the matter was closed.

Despite any faults, my grandfather had a genuine and generous heart, and taught me the importance of hard work and serving others. Whether at church, with the Masons, or just helping a friend or neighbor, he had a silent strength (unless he was angry—no silence there!) that guided those around him. It certainly guided me as he supervised my repairing our house after I accidentally set it on fire. More on this later, since the real lesson was learned from my mother, but my grandfather taught me his own lesson by not judging my actions, but instead focused on teaching me how to make it right. It was best to avoid mistakes, but when they happen, don't waste time and energy fretting on the past. Create solutions that fix the problem and set yourself on a new path to avoid repeating it.

Third, I reflect on my grandmother (my mother's mother). She had a rough life in so many ways, with moments of extreme happiness and extreme pain. The better part of my early childhood was spent with her, and she and I had a unique and somewhat secretive bond that nobody around us could fully appreciate or understand. Among the many lessons I learned from her, some positive and some downright dysfunctional, I learned the importance of a spirit of adventure. She died relatively young (only 61 years old), and had many health challenges, possibly some undiagnosed mental health challenges (or minimally a need for some good counseling), so she never was able to fully experience the adventures of life that she impressed upon me. Her fiery personality, accentuated by her dyed-red hair, was the kind that you loved or hated, but nobody could ever say she wasn't her own woman.

She also taught me acceptance and an appreciation of diversity. Not "diversity" in the modern politically-correct sense of "we are all equal and love everyone and provide everyone with equal respect and opportunity," but in the sense that there is more than one way to live your life, and you can live your life on your own terms in your own unique way, even if others disagree or live differently. There is more than one way to define family, and her role modeling, however dysfunctional, fostered freedom within me to embrace new adventures and non-traditional paths.

I assure you these lessons were not intentional, and in many ways she could be incredibly intolerant, but that was never my personal experience with her. I was her favorite, and at times I would experience some mild guilt over her preferential treatment of me (though even as a child I quickly came to realize these were her issues and not mine). Her youngest son, my uncle, is only four years older than me, so there was this odd almost sibling rivalry between us at times. It was fueled, unintentionally or at least subconsciously, by both my grandmother and my mother. My grandmother could be very vocal and cruel, and her negative treatment of my uncle would create a reaction in my mother that resulted in her overcompensation toward my uncle. My mother would often be far more maternal to my uncle than his own mother was, and my grandmother in turn would manipulate my mother's attention toward my uncle as a sign of diminished care for me, allowing my grandmother to demonstrate her own love for me, implying her love was far superior than that of my own mother. This ended up causing me significant emotional difficulty in adolescence when my grandmother died and I felt abandoned and stuck with what I perceived was lesser quality love from my mother. Then my uncle, still basically a kid himself, moved in with us, into my room, reinforcing my insecurity about my role in my mother's life. When I left for college, my uncle ended up taking over my room, and I felt functionally homeless. This was the icing on the cake of conflict that my mother and I were experiencing at the time. But, I learned tremendous lessons from this as well, and as I advanced in college I came to fully embrace Kohlberg's philosophy that true growth must be borne from conflict. And mine was. (For those not familiar with

Lawrence Kohlberg, he was a psychologist who published famous works on the stages of moral development.)

Last but certainly not least, I reflect on my sister. I was five and a half when my sister was born, but I will never forget that night. I still can close my eyes and remember being woken up in the middle of the night and hearing, "your mother is having the baby."

The rest of that memory plays in slow motion until the moment I held her for the first time. Without her having to do a thing, my sister taught me the lesson of unconditional love. I'm sure I cannot compare the emotions of a five and half year old boy to those of a new parent, but something in me forever changed the moment I held that small beautiful baby in my arms. I knew she was somehow my responsibility and that my selfish world view must change because I was a big brother. My mother would later teach me lessons that would reinforce that feeling, ingraining it into my being, but more on that later.

One moment I have to share because it summarizes this lesson perfectly in a simple and small vignette. My sister and I were only in the same school once, and only for one year. She was in kindergarten and I was in sixth grade. We would walk to school, and periodically run into other neighborhood kids along our journey. That year for Halloween I took my sister around early after school; she was in costume and I was not (my time for trick o' treating would be after dark). We were crossing Merrick Road, in Merrick, New York (on Long Island), and standing in front of the Merrick Marlin restaurant. Waiting for the light to change, some girls from my grade passed us and said to my sister "nice costume."

Of course I can't fully convey the verbal intonation and non-verbal facial expressions in text, but the message being conveyed was not a positive one. It was sarcastic at best, and as they walked away the continued non-verbal expressions bordered on cruel. My sister was going through a chunky phase, as many kids do, and the costume was not particularly flattering (though still very cute). My sister responded to the older girls with a simple and genuine "thank you," not realizing in any way that the complimentary words were anything but.

In retrospect, this scenario is completely indicative of how pre-adolescent kids behave and likely had no impact upon my sister (I doubt she even remembers this ever happened). However, the impact on me was significant, almost damaging. Over three decades later I still cannot fully express the emotions I felt at that moment, and relived at times later. As often is the case, I said nothing at the time, and really didn't even have the opportunity. The light changed and we were crossing the street, the girls long gone in the other direction, before I even had a chance to fully register my disgust.

Once we got back home, and my sister was settled into some interesting activity, I went into my room and cried. I cried out of anger, I cried out of helplessness, I cried out of regret for not doing something, anything. In my mind I was processing all things I should have said or done, but it was too late. This was the first real test of my role as my sister's protector and I failed. Even as I write this now I am still getting teary-eyed. I am also laughing at myself for letting something so insignificant in the big scheme of things bother me so. We were kids, and so were they. I've certainly said and done things far more cruel, so why does this bother me so?

I guess the real life lesson I learned from this incident was that no matter how unconditionally you love someone and no matter how strong your desire to protect that person and shelter the person from harm, even harm unrecognized, there will be moments of helplessness and situations we cannot control. I wasn't prepared to leave my sister alone in that cold cruel world of elementary school without me there to protect her, but I had no choice. My fear was almost crippling, and yet I was so ashamed I couldn't share my feelings with anyone. In fact, I've never really talked much about this until this moment. While junior high provided me with a host of challenges of my own, consuming every ounce of childhood anxiety I had within me, I continued to experience significant internalized pressure and fear about my sister's well-being. I'm not sure if I ever really got over that, and to this day, even though she is married with children and a nice big house and a successful career, there is a part of me that wants to swoop in and solve all her concerns and ensure her happiness. I know I can't really do that, and in this way, despite having no children of my own (well, I have two dogs that I treat like my children), I vicariously experience parenthood through my emotional connection to my siblings, specifically my sister, and now her children. I still can't really talk about this, though. I'm sufficiently comfortable writing it for all the world to read, but I'm not sure if I could ever utter these words from my mouth to her ears. Hopefully she'll read this book and know how much I love her, and her children, even if I don't say it very often.

With due credit given to some of the other people in my life who taught me life lessons, my mother really does deserve the lion's share. She has been a constant and despite having lived away from her for far more years than I ever lived with her, a part of her lives within my thoughts daily. As we both approach ages that were critically important for relatives who came before us, I feel the pressure of time.

# CHAPTER 1

# YOU DIDN'T COME WITH A MANUAL

I was an accident. I guess the more politically correct term is "unplanned." My mother was young and not ready to start a family, but like so many young women in love, things happen. Abortion wasn't legal, but was attainable. Despite changing social mores and a shifting culture toward personal freedom and choice, when presented with the option of an abortion, my mother refused. Despite whatever precautions we may take in life, sometimes actions lead to unintended consequences, but those consequences are your responsibility nonetheless. My mother has never spoken these exact words to me, but she taught me this lesson in so many ways by her words and deeds, and continues to live by this philosophy to this day. But I'm getting ahead of myself. Life lesson number one from my mother is "you didn't come with a manual."

If I had a dollar for every time I heard my mother say "you didn't come with a manual," or the later derivative, "I've done the best I can, but parenthood doesn't come with an instruction manual," I'd be a rich man. I know this is not an earth-shattering revelation, and my mother certainly didn't invent this phrase. I'm sure many people of my generation, and generations before, have heard or felt this. This may not be as true for the Millennial generation and the emerging post-Millennials now populating our educational system since the self-help industry exploded, producing more "how to" and "this and that for dummies" manuals than are probably healthy for society. I'm sure even the tail end of my generation, as I've been labeled "Gen X," experienced the post-Dr. Spock explosion of shifting opinions on the "right" way to raise your children. My childhood slipped by before

1

the "Baby on Board" phenomenon forced us all to feel obligated to protect children to the point of creating protective bubbles around them, and thank goodness because I need my immune system fully developed and functional, not sanitized and encapsulated in a hermetically sealed and manufactured environment.

As children, we seek out our parents and other elders for answers to the never-ending questions we have about life and our world. It was a bit disheartening to learn that my mother didn't have all the answers. My friends' parents seemed to have the answers to their questions, so why didn't my mother borrow their manual? Clearly I was defective and arrived in an incomplete package, so why didn't my mother return me, or refuse the delivery? Hold out until you get the complete model with the manual. Then she let me in on the secret—there is no manual. Nobody comes with one. Some parents may be highly educated, and some may be well-read, but no two models are alike and all those guidebooks can't translate into a perfect parenting strategy.

Don't get me wrong—there are definitely some wrong things parents can do. I've witnessed this time and time again both growing up and in my professional life. But there isn't one right way to raise a child, just a broad spectrum of options that may or may not work in any given situation. I fully own the fact that it is always easier for the couch-potato coach to spout off about how the real coach should be playing the game, so please know it is not my intention to turn this into a book on parenting. I have no children of my own, but I've played at times a significant part in raising thousands of other people's children in the past twenty years, so I feel somewhat qualified to at least reflect on what I see going on around me.

My primary purpose in this book is to reflect on what I learned from my mother, and how those lessons helped shape me into the person I am today. Along the way, I may throw in some of my own commentary, and I won't guarantee that my mother would agree with me. My mother is not perfect, and I am in no way trying to portray her in a saintly light (although she is quick to remind me that she scored a perfect 100 on the New York State Math Regents exam, where I only scored a 99).

We've had some really rough times throughout the years, and there were moments when I wondered if one or the other of us would make it through. However, she is an amazing woman, and for someone who experienced tremendous challenges and struggles throughout her life, she is incredibly optimistic and positively impacts more people's lives than she will ever know. I am yet to visit her even once and not meet someone who feels compelled to share with me how grateful they are to my mother. She doesn't deal well with these types of compliments and is probably mortified that I wrote this book. I hope by the end she will forgive me.

I'm pretty sure my mother would be equally embarrassed to know I talk about her—a lot. While of course she is the inspiration for this book, I've been prodded along for many years by my students and co-workers to write this book. As I share stories, ranging from funny to horrifying, of my life with my mother, people are sometimes shocked, but often impressed (more so impressed that she never killed me). In every class I have ever taught, as I brainstorm for examples to illuminate certain points in the text, my mind naturally wanders to lessons I have learned from my mother. They flow out of me as I lecture—I can't stop them.

Another "aha" moment I first experienced after going away to college and establishing what I felt was my independent sense of self, wholly separate and unique, was how much we really do reflect our parents. The first time a college friend met my mother, he said, "oh, now I understand you." I wasn't sure if that was an insult or a compliment, a commentary on me or on my mother. I pretty much let the comment go at the time, not really wanting to understand it. But as the years progressed and more opportunities arose for people who had only known me in my adult life to then later meet my mother, this exact sentiment repeated itself.

Through the years I've come to take this as a huge compliment, to both of us. I feel like I've turned out pretty well, so for people who hold me in high regard to reflect positively upon my mother makes me feel proud. Even as I describe the lessons I've learned from my mother, I know I've taught her a few along the way. Our symbiotic existence has made both of our lives better and hopefully emanated from each of us in ways that will leave our respective worlds a bit better than we found them. This is my sincere wish for everyone; to live a life in connection with others that generates positive outcomes, no matter how small or large. But I digress, as I tend to do.

So let's get back to that missing manual. I've learned two critical lessons from my mother's incessant use of this phrase. First, there is no roadmap to life, and nobody can tell you exactly what to expect or how to decide what actions are best in any given situation. Despite the best made plans and dreams, as life unfolds things happen beyond your control. Even the strongest desire and will cannot make every detail happen according to a perfect plan. I would give my sister a hard time when she would share her roadmap for the future, which included the age she would be when she got married, had each of her children, etc. I couldn't resist reminding her that there was a critical missing variable in her plans, another person, and even the shrewdest or most manipulative machinations could not guarantee that life would unfold as desired. It was not my desire to burst her bubble, but just create enough of a balanced perspective so she could focus on the things that were truly within her control.

Everyone can offer you opinions, and some may be very informed and valid, and others pure crap. You must rely on yourself to determine what you believe to be the appropriate course of action in any given situation, and then be prepared for the consequences. My mother always did what she believed was best in raising her children, and really in everything in life. Sometimes she got it wrong, but most of the time she got it right. And she was pretty humble and gracious along the way (much more than I have ever been). She was pretty good about explaining the reasons why she would do what she would do, and of course I was that kid who questioned everything.

She did her best to resist the easy response of, "because I said so," despite her obvious frustration when I would negotiate ad nauseam for my desired outcome. On a few rare occasions during the "bad years" I got a slap or two, but in retrospect had I been her I would have likely locked me in a cage and gone out drinking. Luckily I have dogs and can do that without getting arrested. She seldom invoked the "I'm the mother and that's why" stance, but also didn't devolve into a lengthy "let's process everything" approach, nor did she seek to be my friend in lieu of a mother. She gave me enough latitude to learn without prescription.

While there is no roadmap to life, that is no excuse for not planning. Even if nothing works out as intended, you'll get more accomplished with a plan than without one, understanding that you need sufficient flexibility to adjust the plan as you go. The art of adjusting the plan, and even one step further and making the unintended seem as though it all happened as it should, is a gift my mother passed along to me. For my mother, I think much of this was grounded in faith.

The second critical lesson is that, even though life comes without a manual, it is no excuse for not trying to gather all the information you can and create one as you go. My mother is highly supportive of education, through both formal and informal means. Despite what resources we did or did not have at our disposal, she would make any necessary personal sacrifice to ensure that my sister and I had the best opportunities possible. She didn't just give us whatever we wanted, and definitely made sure we understand the contributions we needed to make to our own success, but I'll get more into that later. I was also always impressed that my mother would support things she didn't always understand. As kids often do, we would become obsessed with one whim or another. The burden still fell to us to explain how our desired whim would be beneficial, but she would find ways to support the things that really mattered most to us.

I know it was never her intention to turn me into a geeky over-analytical researcher, but the signs were there pretty early on. My mother did her best to temper it, but I had the gift of persuasion and knew how to schmooze adults in ways that would impress them. I tended to communicate more freely and comfortably with adults rather than my peers. This would often lead to my mother's commentary about how if they all really knew what a handful I was they might think differently of me, but luckily they didn't and I had no intention of letting that cat out of the bag. I think she secretly admired that about me, though it made raising me much more difficult.

A perfect example of this is the time in elementary school when there was heightened awareness of peanut allergies in children, so the school created a policy banning peanut butter and jelly sandwiches. I believe I was in the third grade. Every day I ate a peanut butter and jelly sandwich. I was not happy, and wasn't going to accept this. I smuggled in my peanut butter and jelly sandwiches, and in personal protest would sneak under the lunchroom table to eat. Naturally I got caught and was instructed to cease and desist. Not a chance.

I went to the library and researched the issue, and chatted with the school nurse to see how much of a problem this alleged peanut allergy situation was really causing in our specific elementary school (confidentiality laws weren't really enforced in the 70s). I then proceeded to the principal's office to have a discussion.

The woman in the front office wasn't quite sure what to make of this. She contacted my teacher, who informed her it was best to just let me see the principal since I wasn't likely to go away. After a lovely chat with the principal, and presenting my research and concerns, the principal agreed that maybe the policy was too hasty and restrictive, and agreed to change the policy back, allowing me to peacefully enjoy my peanut butter and jelly sandwiches once more in public.

The principal called my mother at work to let her know the problem had been resolved. My mother wasn't aware of the problem to begin with. Back in the day, teachers were naive enough to believe sending a note home with a kid ensured the parent would receive it. If I didn't like the content of the message, why cause undue stress for my mother by sharing the note? She would have been likely to forbid me to bring my peanut butter and jelly sandwiches to school, and where would that have left me! I then would have had to sneak the sandwich both out of the house and in to the school, and that was more ruse than a third grader should have to endure.

The principal proceeded to inform my mother of how proud she should be. She had to stop him in his tracks and inquire who was running this school. As she relayed this story to me later, she asked the principal how a young child could march into his office and change school policy. She also informed him that he was creating a monster, and he didn't realize what she was going to have to put up with at home from me. While she was right, at the same time I know she was proud. Well, minimally impressed. As Mom and I processed my actions, she expressed the expected concern, but also incredible support. She reinforced the value of following your passion and maneuvering through the appropriate channels to enact change, after conducting the necessary research to support your desired change. Basically, you better know what you are saying and have thought out all the possible scenarios before you open your mouth.

True, I didn't come with a manual. Even if I had, it probably would have been obsolete by pre-school. In my early adulthood when I fully realized what a difficult child I was to raise, I would joke that my mother should write a manual for other parents facing similarly challenging children. While my mother never codified the manual, she has certainly passed along the wisdom to many frustrated parents struggling with difficult children, especially ill-mannered teens. She's even encouraged some really defeated parents at the end of their rope to talk with me. We've both shared lots of crazy stories, and helped others laugh and cry as they struggled through the confusing maze that is parenthood. Maybe this book can provide a rough draft for that manual.

# CHAPTER 2

# NEED VERSUS WANT

"I want, I want, I want . . ." Oh the familiar whine, frequently heard from children, and sometimes heard from adolescents and adults. But, something interesting starts to happen as children grow into pre-teens: the use of the term "want" tends to shift to the use of the term "need." Somehow kids wise up and learn that a "need" sounds more important than a "want," and the more emphatic the insistence of the "need," the more likely they are to get their way. The challenge is that kids don't typically define need and want in the same way as adults, and the more I deal with parents of the Millennial generation, the more I find the lines between the two blurring even for the parents.

As far back as I can remember, my mother was pretty clear in making sure I understood the difference. She never read me any dictionary definitions of these terms, but let's take a look at Webster's for some insight. A need is "a physiological or psychological requirement for the well-being of an organism." A want is "a desire, a wish, or demand." So following these descriptions, it is safe to say we NEED food, shelter, safety, clothing, education, and maybe even some social interaction. However, we don't NEED gourmet food, a McMansion, haute couture, private tutors or academies, or a full-time security guard to monitor our every move and escort us to every activity in our lives (also known as over-protective or helicopter parents). Naturally needs may change over time, such as the level of need for care of an infant compared to the level of need for care for an adolescent or young adult.

While some parents feel the need to satisfy their children's every desire, my mother was quick to educate me on the fallacy of this parental approach. Providing for your children everything they need is admirable and many may believe it is a parent's obligation to do so. If a parent has the means and capacity to satisfy every need for a child this can be wonderful, though the reality of life is that children will have needs that may be beyond a parent's recognition and the parent will likely never be able to satisfy every need. But, receiving everything a child wants can diminish his or her appreciation of those very things that were intended to make the child happy, leaving a perpetually unsatisfied child and most likely a perpetually unsatisfied adult. A critical part of seeking what we want in life is learning how to acquire those things for ourselves. The process of earning those things we desire is part and parcel in achieving the satisfaction that those things may bring. When we are handed everything we want, it means nothing. Despite a parent's best intentions, the unfortunate outcome may be quite the contrary.

Don't get me wrong. There is nothing wrong with wants. In fact, if it weren't for wants, we may not possess the motivation to continuously improve ourselves and others. However, what level of obligation do, or should, others have to satisfy our wants? My mother has worked hard her entire life to ensure that the needs of those who were her responsibility by circumstance or choice were met. When possible, she might also seek to provide for people's wants, but I always understood that she was under no obligation to do so. My mother has a very generous nature, and frequently engages in community service and donating to causes she values. She made sure to instill this sense of obligation to help others in her children. This was a foundational aspect of the lesson of need versus want. No matter how much or how little we had, there were always others who had less and had a greater need than ours.

My mother demonstrated this ethic of care for us in many ways, but three distinct examples are clear in my mind. First, from the time I was a very small child, my mother would bring me to church every week, including attending Sunday school. She insisted I contribute something every week, even if only a penny, to the offering. My mother personally believes in tithing, and would encourage us to do the same, but it was ultimately our choice how much we chose to contribute. All she required was that we contribute something because we could and we should. As I got older and my interests diversified, she respected my choice to contribute to the causes that I personally valued, even if they weren't her causes. Even though I initially began donating to church because my mother made me, and I didn't want to get in trouble, in time I came to donate because I wanted her respect and didn't want to disappoint her. As I became an adult, I continued to donate because it was fully my choice, desire, and I believe obligation, to do so; no longer because of my mother's insistence. But would I have made those same choices as an adult had I not been "forced" to do so by my mother as a kid? Maybe, maybe not, but I'm glad I'll never have to know.

Second, every week my mother would take me to the local nursing home and we would play bingo with the residents. Most of the residents were very elderly, with various disabilities, and limited communication capacity. The place smelled like urine, and it was not uncommon to encounter the source material in the hallways, bingo room, or on the residents themselves. I really didn't enjoy going at first, but my mother would take me to Carvel or Friendly's for ice cream afterward, so it seemed like a necessary evil to acquire what I really wanted.

While the smell and presence of urine never diminished, my sensitivity to it did, and in time I developed relationships with many of the residents. When possible, I would regularly gravitate toward certain residents, and if my favorite residents were sick and couldn't come that Monday night, I would miss them. Some of the more able residents would knit things for us, and we would bring flowers or plants from time to time to brighten up their rooms.

Each Monday night our routine would be the same: we would play bingo and get ice cream. It was after bingo one night as we were getting back in the car to go get ice cream, that my mother just sat in silence for a moment and didn't start the car. As calmly as she could, doing her best to maintain her composure, she informed me and my sister that she and my father were getting a divorce. I was almost ten.

My sister was too young to really understand what was going on. My mother and I both made a valiant effort to fight back any tears, and even though little more was said, I understood our lives would forever change. We continued our Monday night bingo throughout the separation and after the divorce, but I noticed my mother wasn't getting ice cream anymore. She would say she didn't want any, but kids are much more attentive and intuitive than adults think. As the money got tighter, my mother had the difficult conversation with us that we just couldn't get ice cream after bingo every week anymore. Especially since I was getting older, my mother said she would understand if I didn't want to come to bingo anymore, but it wasn't about the ice cream anymore. I wanted to go, and I felt the residents needed me to go. Since my sister hadn't quite reached this point yet being five and half years younger than me, I was happy to sacrifice my ice cream so she could still get her incentive to tolerate the urine smell. Even at her young age, my sister quickly caught the spirit of volunteering and shared our desire to be there every Monday night, ice cream or no ice cream.

Third, my mother made us sing in the church choir, at least initially. I'm sure part of her rationale was to keep us busy doing productive things and help keep us out of trouble. But that wasn't the only reason. My mother also wanted us to develop an appreciation for music, and learn for ourselves what talents we might (or might not) possess. Once we determined for ourselves if the choir was something we enjoyed, she would let us choose to continue or not, as long as we replaced that activity with some other productive activity that would help us develop a skill set or determine an area of talent or interest. She encouraged us to take advantage of every opportunity we could to learn as much as we could about our interests, desires, and talents. As our natural proclivities emerged, the "other shoe dropped," so to speak.

"So what do you plan to do with this new-found talent?" my mother would ask.

You mean it's not just enough to find out we like doing something and just do it for ourselves and for fun?

11

"Well, sure, you could, but why wouldn't you want to share your talents with others? Would you really want to deny the world of enjoying the things that you've come to enjoy?"

With the developing ego of a child being what it is, how could my sister and I not want to share these great talents that had made our mother so proud? So, growing up we wouldn't just sing in the choir, but we would sing carols for neighborhood shut-ins, and sing at the nursing home, and teach the younger children how to read music and learn to sing the songs we would sing. And the same was true for everything we did. Mom would apply this across all areas of our lives: "It's great that you are good in math, so you probably should help tutor the other kids who aren't as good as you are."

Mom wasn't one to harp on things, and I really don't recall her saying these things that often. What I really remember is her DOING these things. She would never ask us to do anything she wouldn't be willing to do herself, and most the time she didn't even have to ask us. She would just do the things she would do and role model for us what she expected, or at least hoped, we would do. Sometimes I would question my mother about why she did some of the things she did, and she would reply "because I can." If there was ever a way my mother could help, she did.

As I got older and started contemplating my career path is when my mother would engage me more in discussion about how I intended to use my talents to help others and improve the world. Personal success was of course important and encouraged, but we always knew it was never just about us. Paraphrasing the Bible, my mother reinforced for us that "to whom much is given much is required," and she made sure we understood how fortunate we were and the obligation this fortune engendered.

Another one of my mother's rules was that we would attend church and Sunday school weekly and complete all of the requirements for our Confirmation class, right up until the point of getting confirmed. I was raised United Methodist, and Confirmation is when we became a free-standing independent member of the church. Our Christening is when our parents declared their intentions for us, but to me, Confirmation was serious adult business. Growing up on the south shore of Long Island, New York, I had many Jewish friends (and some Jewish relatives), and envied the significance of the Bar Mitzvah. Many of my Christian friends went through the motions, but didn't really treat their Confirmation as any big deal. It was a huge deal to me, and largely because of my mother. Not because she stressed it in any particular way above and beyond any other ritual of our religion per se, but because she let the Confirmation and my spiritual life beyond that point be my own choice.

She believed as a child I needed religion, but as a transitioning adult (or the religious equivalent thereof) it was up to me to want religion, and want this particular religion, on my own and not simply as something I inherited from her. In retrospect, that is a pretty big risk, or leap of faith, to take with an eighth grader. I made my Confirmation, and continued to attend church, Sunday school, youth group, and choir practice every week until I left for college, long past when my mother required it. I knew she wanted me to get Confirmed and stay active in the church, but she needed me to want it or feel I needed it for myself.

Speaking of my Confirmation, as I mentioned, many of my friends and classmates were Jewish and had celebrated very elaborate (and often expensive) Bar and Bat Mitzvahs. My mother struggled to be able to afford to keep us living in a home that was in a good public school district, but she couldn't afford to compete with the lifestyle of many of my classmates. Between seventh and eighth grade, I attended so many wonderful parties, and I wanted to host a comparable party to celebrate my Confirmation. I knew we couldn't afford a party to rival those of my friends (many of which cost the same as a wedding), but my mother knew how much it meant to me. I may not have needed a party, but my mother knew I needed to feel that my Confirmation meant as much as any other religious rite of passage, and that I needed to feel that I was just as good as any of my peers, despite our comparably diminished means.

What my mother lacked in cash she made up for in ingenuity and creativity. There was a nice marina clubhouse near where my grandparents lived and they knew the owner. My mother's best friend was dating a chef, who agreed to cater the party at cost. Instead of purchasing fancy favors we bought some wholesale items and put the favors together ourselves (which also created some nice quality time for me, my mother, and my sister). It was a high-class party on a more affordable budget. I know there were many other things on which my mother needed to spend that money, but she wanted to give me this party. I told you she wasn't perfect—she amended her own "needs and wants" rules, and in the process taught me another important lesson—some wants are more important than needs. It was one of the best nights of my life, despite very bad weather and my bedroom getting flooded (I lived in the basement).

My mother's ethic of care, as exemplified in these three examples, focused on how she used her time, her talents, and her gifts. She never used these words in this way, but her actions clearly communicated these values. It is interesting to me that I heard so many pastors over the years preach the need for us to contribute our gifts, our time, and our talents, and those words had minimal if any impact on me. Yet, my mother never preached these words to me but simply lived them, and I received that message loud and clear. This also taught me another important lesson that would serve me well in my work with college students—I can't just talk a good talk. I need to lead by example and engage my students in their own learning.

Probably the most important lesson that I learned from my mother related to the need versus want continuum is the difference between equality and equity. Later in life I would ponder upon the meaning of these words from an academic perspective, mostly applied to social justice theories, diversity, civil rights, and the like. That is not how my mother was thinking about it. How I really learned the difference between equality and equity was while going back-to-school shopping with my mother and my sister. My mother always had a budget, and we understood what our parameters were. I'll talk more about this in the next chapter.

Even more important than the amount of money in the budget, was how it was subdivided. Back to school shopping always began with a thorough inventory of what we already had. Which items of clothing still fit, which didn't (we'd just have to get over the fact that our schoolmates might be mortified that our clothing was from "last season" or earlier). What supplies did we need, etc. From that came the shopping list of essentials that we needed to successfully begin the new school year.

As kids, we were more focused on equality. If I just bought a new pair of shoes that cost $25.00, then my sister would think she should have $25.00 to spend on herself, and vice versa. My mother was quick to point out that was what we wanted, but back to school shopping was about what we needed. If I needed a new pair of shoes, then I would get them, but if my sister only needed a new dress and her dress cost less (or more) than my shoes, then that was all she would get. My mother believed in need-based budgeting. This approach meant my sister and I were not always treated equally, but we each had our needs met, and this was how we perceived equity.

The same principle applied to many things in our home growing up. My sister and I were different ages, with different interests, talents, and hence different needs. My sister and I both found fault with my mother's application of equity at various times.

"Why can Michael stay up later than me?" my sister would ask.

"Because he is older, and doesn't need as much sleep at his age as you need at yours," my mother would reply.

"Why can Jennifer get away with acting out like that and I can't?" I would protest.

"Because you are older and you should know better. Even if she hits you, you cannot correct her action by hitting her back because you are bigger and stronger than she is and you will hurt her. She is not hurting you, she is really just trying to get your attention," my mother would explain.

In unison, both children singing as if in the chorus, "but that's not fair!"

I can hear my mother now: "Life's not fair, so it is better not to create unrealistic expectations for you now that will just create a lifetime of disappointment and frustration later."

Maybe my mother would get a bit too profound at times for the likes of young children, but she was absolutely right and her equity-oriented approach to parenting saved me a lot of heartache and frustration throughout my adolescence and early adulthood. I can't tell you how many times I would remind myself that life is not fair, we aren't all created exactly the same, so I shouldn't expect equal reactions and equal treatment from everyone in life, nor should I respond in equal measure. But I have always strived for equity, and in doing so I was able to get my needs met and help satisfy the needs of others, even if our wants went unfulfilled.

I realize, and so does my mother, that life is not that simple. The individual and social struggles of equality versus equity, and need versus want, cannot be tied up so neatly with a bow. Of course there are times when equality matters. If I am grading a test for my students they expect and deserve a grading matrix that is equally applied to all, regardless of ability or effort. Will some students who didn't even study for the test end up with an A, and some who really tried end up with a D? Sure. Life's not fair.

But what do I do about it? I treat my students equitably in the effort to teach them, and help them have the reality check that they cannot all approach my class in the same way. Learning is a collaborative effort, and it is my job to work with my students so we can collectively determine what they each need to succeed. I learned this from my mother. Success is not defined the same for everyone, so equivalent expectations, chores, etc., were not set for me and my sister; however, there was equity.

As I wrap up this chapter, I need to give a "shout out" to my stepfather. He and my mother married while I was finishing up high school, so I didn't live with them for that long. My sister lived with them much longer, and a couple of his children (all older than me) had the opportunity to live in the house on breaks from college or between college and the start of a full-time career. I imagine if he is reading this chapter he is probably thinking I am giving my mother a bit too much credit for strictly enforcing a philosophy of need versus want, particularly with my sister.

My mother had her soft moments and would from time to time give in with me, but overall I believe she held pretty firm and when I really needed it, she provided the tough love that seems to have dissipated a good bit in the Millennial parenting style. My stepfather was able to provide her with the extra support she may have needed from time to time to stay the course with me, and that was challenging to do given how argumentative I could be. My stepfather is likely too polite to point out, so I'll do it for him, that my mother "fell off the wagon" a bit with my sister as she entered adolescence. In the end, my mother always found her compass, and my sister and I are the better for it.

As every parent knows, especially those who have multiple children spread across a period of time, family circumstances and dynamics can change over time. I was born closer to the front end of Generation X, and in my early childhood spent a good bit of time with my maternal grandmother, so I may have picked up some Baby Boomer generational traits that my younger sister did not. I also have far more vivid memories of my parents' divorce, my grandparents' funerals, and the financially lean years while my mother struggled as a single parent working a very demanding management-level job in a very unforgiving corporate setting. I remember my mother leaving before dawn and returning after dark, and some of the burdens of child and household care falling to me at what by modern standards would be considered far too early an age. Now that I'm old enough to have watched relatives, friends, and colleagues raise children through adolescence and begin sending them off to college or the workforce, I'm realizing why many people my age have the life skills we have and some people in these latter generations do not.

I don't blame my mother for the shift in life circumstances, and I certainly can't blame her for the significant cultural shifts of the 70s, 80s and 90s. Life's not fair after all, and she prepared me well to handle that reality. I also have to take responsibility for part of the shift in parenting style as my mother transitioned from raising both me and my sister, to just raising my sister. I was a pain in the ass. I was too smart for my own good, wildly impatient, and never really accepted that I wasn't an adult from birth. My mother and I had some terrible arguments, and I was not one for losing a good argument.

At the height of my "difficult phase" when I simply would not shut up, there was an incident when my mother had me by the shoulders and was shaking me as hard as she could at the top of the stairs that led to our basement. She looked deeply in my eyes and shouted, "I am going to throw you down these stairs. I would rather go to jail than listen to you for one more minute!"

I got the message, but still wanting the upper hand. I looked her back in her eyes and said as calmly as possible, "If that will make you feel better, do what you have to do."

In frustration she let me go and retreated to her bedroom. I won that battle, but she ultimately won the war. She managed to get me through high school and into college without killing me, and that is a pretty significant accomplishment.

Back to my sister, she was pretty and popular and smart and a really good child. I mean too good. Sure she acted up from time to time like all children do, but up until the point when I was leaving for college, she had pretty much been the perfect kid. The dynamics of gender stereotyping aside, she didn't seem to need the same level of parental effort that I did. Maybe that created a false sense of security in my mother, coupled with my mother's professional success which generated a growing level of financial means. Add to that the very difficult relationship between me and my mother at the time, and my sister looked like a golden child. As my high school years continued, I grew to hate that school and everyone in it. I was ready to leave and was determined to do everything in my power to get out of New York tout de suite.

Despite some of my bad habits, like cutting school, calling the office and pretending to be my stepfather, and forging sick notes with his signature, I had great grades and was able to earn early admission to Emory University in Atlanta, Georgia. In my junior year I decided I had had enough, and decided to jumpstart my college education a year early. I was 16 years old when I entered college, and 19 years old when I graduated Emory with my Bachelor's degree. There were definitely moments I teetered on the edge of success or failure, and now can recognize those moments in my students.

Even the morning I left for college was a calamity. Having overslept, it took a mad rush in what felt like a high-speed car chase to get me to LaGuardia airport in time to catch my flight. No big hugs or teary goodbyes, just my mother abruptly proclaiming, "Get out!"

I arrived in Atlanta, but my luggage did not. So I sat for hours with my typewriter and pillow awaiting my luggage. I called my mother to share that I arrived safely and expressed my frustration over being stuck in the airport, to which she coolly exclaimed, "and who's fault is that?" She always had a way of cutting to the chase with a much needed reality check.

I pretty much figured my mother was done with me, and to be honest, at that moment, I was pretty much done with her, and just about everyone else from my "old" life. I was ready for college and a new life in a new city, far away from everyone and everything I had previously known. I made a few obligatory calls home, and had a few moments of panic when I realized everyone at college was as smart as me (or smarter) and my intellectual standing quickly diminished from "the top tier" to "about average."

My mother was always gracious, but I didn't really sense that she missed me. I didn't blame her given the horrors of the previous years, so in our ways we each moved on. My mother's focus now shifted to my sister and correcting the perceived mistakes she must have made with me for me to be such a horrible teenager. I believed my mother considered me a "lost cause" at this point, and years later she admitted to me that she wasn't sure if I'd make it away at college at 16. She always hoped for my success, but a part of her feared I'd crash and burn. There is a fine line between genius and insanity after all. Not wanting to "lose" my sister in the same way, my mother let the need versus want pendulum swing a bit too far to the want end of the continuum for a while.

This really hit home for me when I was visiting from college and my mother asked me to take my sister shopping for new socks. My sister had my mother's credit card, so my only role was to get my sister there and back safely, and call her at work should the store give us a hard time using the credit card. At that same age, my mother would have told me to catch the bus, but my sister being a girl was a bit more sheltered. I was also a bit shocked that my sister even had my mother's credit card, especially without any additional parameters or limitations.

We arrived at the little boutique where my sister wanted to purchase socks. Where were we? I thought socks were something that came in a six or twelve pack from the flea market, or if desperate and there was no time to get to the flea market, from Sear's, the five and dime, or even from the grocery or drug store. Who knew such stores even existed.

We entered the store and headed toward the fancy display filled with more colors and styles of socks than my mind could fathom. My sister starts contemplating and selecting a rainbow of these fat thick socks called "EGs," apparently named after some guy who's initials were "EG" (Eric something?) and who's signature appeared on the bottom of the sock. Some pairs even came in boxes with a picture of this bald guy, presumably "EG."

Get ready for the real craziness! We go to check out, and the bill for about a dozen pairs of socks is over $200! The "plain" ones cost $18 a pair and the "fancy" ones ranged from $22-$24 a pair (and remember this was in the 1980's). My entire back to school budget for clothes at that same age was about half of what my sister just spend on SOCKS!

Before we swipe my mother's credit card and present the signed note authorizing my sister to use the card, I thought it would be prudent to call my mother and verify that she truly had lost her mind and was letting my sister buy $200 in socks. Lo and behold, the universe had indeed imploded. "Your sister needs new socks, and those are the ones she wants" my mother said, sounding annoyed that I was bothering her at work.

What? Need and want being so frivolously expressed in the same sentence, by MY mother? Clearly things had changed after my departure. I guess I was partially to blame. I adored my baby sister and contributed to the construction of the bubble of protection and comfort that made her believe she needed an $18 pair of socks. I even remember how my mother and I pushed her first Cabbage Patch doll upon her since we had heard they were all the rage. She initially thought they were ugly (and they were). Of course by Christmas they truly were all the rage and my sister eventually jumped on the band wagon, which meant my mother paid over $100 for a doll she could have purchased six months earlier when she wanted to for only $20. If we pushed my sister into falling in love with a baby with a guy's signature on its butt, why should I be surprised that years later she would want to wear socks with some guy's signature on her heel?

Fret not, my sister's story also has a happy ending. Through some gentle prodding from her new husband, my mother's compass got back on track, and need and want slowly but surely returned to balance. Like I had in my youth, my sister got a job (actually multiple jobs), and learned that my mother would provide for her needs and she would have to earn her own money to provide for her wants. My sister has impeccable taste, and likes really nice things. She is willing to work really hard and make sacrifices in other areas to acquire those things, and that is her choice. But she too has a very generous nature. Even as a teenager, working multiple jobs, she would spend much more than I thought was prudent on nice gifts for our younger half-siblings. Since I was gone, it was now her opportunity to play big sibling.

At work, I have the opportunity to speak to parents and students at college orientation, and one of the frequent agenda items is need versus want. I often ask my students how many of them have iPhones, late model cars, new laptops, etc. The majority do. I ask them if they need these things. They respond that they do. This is when my mother swoops in.

"So you perceive that you need a cell phone, and maybe you do. But do you NEED an iPhone or the newest smart phone, and the monthly bill that goes with it? Would a $20 "go phone" from WalMart with a basic voice plan not meet the need? Sure it would, but not the want. Do you need a car? Maybe, but do you need a loaded current year SUV with a monthly payment that exceeds your monthly rent? No."

I sense my students don't appreciate this conversation.

Even with the parents, I'll ask difficult questions, like "Does your student WANT to come home on weekends and hang out with a high school sweetheart? Sure. But your student NEEDS to stay here at school, make new friends, study, and get connected to this new university environment in order to succeed in college and not fall into a rut of 13th grade. Does your student WANT to switch rooms because she is uncomfortable with her new roommate who looks and acts differently from her, listens to different music, so it is easier to avoid conflict and just get out? Sure. But what she NEEDS is for you to make her stay and work through the conflict, learning how to solve her own problems, and communicate with people who are different from her."

Often I sense the parents don't appreciate the conversation much more than their kids do.

There is almost no day that goes by when working with college students and/or their parents that I can avoid a discussion of need versus want, and I wonder how they made it this far without having confronted this dichotomy on their own. I've met many parents who invested a great deal of time in being friends with their children, and I appreciate the value of the close relationships that many of my students have with their parents compared to previous generations. However, some failed to invest equally in being a parent, and realize the error too late, or fail to see it at all and want to shift the burden of responsibility for solving problems to a third party.

Some will likely reflect more seriously upon these decisions when they want to retire but realize they need to keep working because their grown children still live at home with them and/or don't have sufficient independent financial means to care for themselves, more or less provide any kind of assistance to their parents in their old age should they need it. Blame the economy all you want, but the signs of these behaviors and challenges were vividly apparent long before the bottom fell out. We may not want to discuss and confront this, but we need to.

# CHAPTER 3

# MONEY

You can't successfully live in a capitalistic democracy and not have some understanding of how money works. Money has always been a part of my life, and there has never been a time when money management was not part of my education. At times I've had none, and at times I've had plenty, but the principles I've used to manage what I had I learned from my mother. She made sure I understood that money is a means to an end. Money in and of itself has no value unless you have a clear sense of what you need (or want) to acquire with that money. Money buys things, but can also buy security, status, and support. But money is not the only way to acquire that which you need or desire. The lack of financial means can generate tremendous creativity and collaboration. My mother's lessons on money always included goal setting and needs assessment. While I didn't realize it at the time, these lessons would be of significant benefit to my future employers who would come to enjoy the fruits of my conservative fiscal management and creative means of generating resources. I'm sure my mother wasn't the only source of this skill set, but she certainly solidified the foundation.

There are so many great examples to share. I'll begin with the Christmas Club. A January tradition in my home was the annual trip to the bank to set up the Christmas Club. The same way my mother insisted that I make a weekly contribution to the church offering, she also insisted that I always make a weekly contribution to myself through a Christmas Club savings account. As she explained, it served a number of purposes. First, it forced you to create savings and get in the habit of living on a bit less than you earn. Second, it helped you have a more substantial pot of resources at a time when you would need it most, to buy Christmas gifts, without having to generate future debt. Third, it gave you the opportunity to know far in advance exactly what your shopping budget would be, allowing you to plan what you wanted to purchase for who, and keep an eye out for bargains so you could stretch your budget even further.

My mother never got into complex lectures about the value of money over time, how different types of financial instruments worked, or how to shop around for the best interest rates, but the process of selecting a Christmas Club savings account each January, making my weekly contributions all year long, watching my passbook balance increase and my monthly interest credit applied and compounded, and reaping the benefits of that account each December when I had my shopping list ready and the necessary resources to complete my desired purchases, taught me far more than any lengthy lecture could have.

The Christmas Club money was also a huge boost for my self-esteem and sense of independence. The idea of buying a gift for a parent and having that parent pay for her or his own gift seemed counterintuitive to me. I also resented the control someone else had over you when that individual ultimately made the decision on what you could and could not give. One year I wanted to buy my mother a small Hummel figurine. She collected these cherubic characters but had to grow her collection very slowly because of the high cost. Even the smallest figurines could range in price from $50 to $150 when I was a kid, and my entire annual Christmas Club initially was barely over $50. If I would have asked my mother or father or even a grandparent to purchase that level of gift on my behalf I would have been immediately shut down. However, the Christmas Club money was all mine, and how I chose to use it was also mine. Some years I made what others perceived as foolish choices, but I always felt good about having the freedom to choose (and a good public transit system that provided a means of independence).

I'm sure you are wondering where the money came from that I contributed to the church each week and to my Christmas Club savings account. Initially it came from my mother in the form of an allowance. My mother would generate a list of chores that I was responsible for completing each week, and assuming they were completed satisfactorily, I would receive my allowance. To also help me learn time management, my mother would help me schedule when my chores should occur, and had me calculate the amount of time those chores took me to complete. Based on my rate of weekly allowance, I was able to determine what my approximate hourly wage earned was, and the level of effort necessary to acquire various things I wanted. If I wanted a book that cost $1, and my hourly allowance rate was roughly twenty-five cents, then I knew I had to work four hours to earn that book. The value of that book took on a whole new meaning for me, and when I would finally acquire that book, the experience of reading it was somehow more satisfying because I knew the labor I contributed. I also tended to take pretty good care of my things because I knew what they were worth and the effort involved in their acquisition.

As I got older, my mother also helped me appreciate the level of effort others contributed to the creation of the things we had. When opportunities arose for me to earn income from sources outside of my own home, my mother would encourage me to do so. Whether it was performing small tasks for relatives or neighbors, or working a "real job," there was always an expectation that in life we all had to earn our keep. My first "real job" was stocking shoes off the books since I was too young to work legally. I made less than minimum wage, but wasn't paying any taxes yet . . . except to my mother. Another one of my mother's rules was that once you had a "real job" you had to contribute financially to the household. She didn't tell me at the time that she was putting all that money into savings for my own benefit later when I was likely to really need it more than a young teen thinks he needs whatever he thinks he needs at that moment.

There were some negative unintended consequences to my mother's approach to teaching me responsible money and time management. I definitely inherited my mother's creativity and work ethic, and in the sixth grade I became aware of an entrepreneurial opportunity in my school. I noticed some of the popular kids would bring in boxes of lollipops or bags of gum to share with their friends.

These items were not available on the school grounds, and were generally discouraged but not outright banned. The popular kids weren't inclined to share with the unpopular kids, and us "poorer" kids (again, a relative term of perception when dealing with wealthier peers), couldn't necessarily afford to purchase and provide treats to each other.

One day when shopping at the flea market, I noticed a big box of Blow Pops on sale. It was my intention to purchase a new shirt, but a light bulb came on in my head. If I could buy a box of 50 Blow Pops for about $3.00, that was about six cents a lollipop. The local stores around school would sell them for twenty-five cents per lollipop. I could sell them to my classmates for a dime, undercutting the local competition but still making a profit. Even the "poorer" kids could swing a dime (Do you really need that milk at lunch? Wouldn't an afternoon Blow Pop be so much better!), and the unpopular kids would be an easy sell so they could engage in the same activities as the popular kids, and none would be any the wiser about how they acquired their new found treat. In my own way I could even the social playing field and make money doing it!

The Blow Pops were a huge hit, and I could easily sneak them into school in my backpack and take advantage of recess or other small breaks when the teacher was otherwise occupied with another activity. After sixth grade I moved on to junior high school, a new school with many new students. In junior high was this cool thing called homeroom, and approximately every forty-five minutes we would get to change classes and have about eight minutes to wonder the hallways taking a restroom break, visiting our lockers, and getting to our next class. I also transitioned from a walker in elementary school, to a bus rider in junior high school. This transition from sixth to seventh grade significantly expanded my market horizons.

I wasn't limited to a couple of clandestine sales opportunities each day, but now had numerous periods to conduct business, a larger client base with customers changing hourly, and my very own store front to expand my on-hand inventory (oh yeah, and keep some books, a coat, etc.). I also became quickly involved in co-curricular activities, opening up an entire after-school market. Since my school ended earlier than my sister's, and she participated in her own afterschool program, I could still fulfill my household responsibilities and enjoy all these great new opportunities of my own.

The Blow Pop business was good, and it didn't take me long to learn another important lesson about money: supply and demand. There were many vendors near my elementary school who sold the same product I did, which fueled the need for me to undercut their prices. My junior high was located in a more residential area, and it was a much further walk to the nearest deli to purchase snacks. We weren't allowed to leave the school grounds between classes, so the nearby supply was scarce, and the demand for my product increased. So I raised my prices. Most kids had quarters anyway, and making change was a pain, so I took a risk and jumped from a dime to a quarter. I also increased my product line when I realized lots of kids liked the gum, but didn't want to mess with the lollipop. I was able to buy packs of gum in 10-pack sleeves for about a buck. I sold my entire inventory for a quarter an item, making a handsome profit. The gum sales ended up surpassing the lollipop sales, so I started offering volume purchase incentives. For $1.00, I'd throw in an extra lollipop for free. The five for one dollar deal was hot, and actually made my life much easier. Instead of lugging heavy bags of change home from school and rolling quarters, then carrying heavy shoeboxes of quarters to the bank or A&P to convert to dollars, my customers were doing the exchange labor for me. I quickly put the gum on the same deal, and expanded the variety of my inventory to include different types of gum. To encourage up sales to the even dollar, I allowed product mixing.

The "select any five for a buck" campaign was a little too successful. I noticed a few other kids trying to cut in on my action, and some were willing to sell for twenty cents. Those foolish kids would learn the backbreaking effort of carrying all those dimes, and needing to have lots of nickels on hand to make change for a quarter, and typically folded as quickly as they arose. One of them approached me about a merger, but I had a great thing going, I didn't trust him, and honestly I was getting a little greedy. In eighth grade I did add a couple of trusted friends with some satellite lockers who assisted me in covering some of the different hallways and class tracks (I was in the gifted program, so I didn't have sufficient coverage of the "average" classes, which were larger than mine). For a modest cut of the profits, my two friends helped grow my little business, but in doing so we gained the attention of the school administration.

Evidently we were breaking school rules (not to mention the law since I wasn't reporting my income in any way), and despite my most persuasive oratory pleas, I couldn't win this one. "The Candy Man" as some had come to call me was no more. The retirement of my little home-grown business was sad, but also reduced a great deal of stress that I hadn't fully realized I was experiencing. My junior high included grades seven through nine, and in tenth grade I entered another new school, high school. I revived my candy business in my new school. Even though I knew my academic record followed me into high school, I was hoping my student disciplinary record did not, and I could claim ignorance of the school rules should I get caught again. Well, it did, and I did, and the trouble was a bit more severe, but at least I turned a nice profit while it lasted.

Upon my second and final retirement from the candy business, I knew I needed a real job. That is what led me to the shoe store, since I had heard through a girlfriend that they would pay me under the table until I could work legally. Once I was of age, the shoe store was only willing to move me just above minimum wage, and after taxes, it was about what I was making before. The Wendy's around the corner from my house was hiring, and paying a good bit above minimum wage. The restaurant was open more hours than the shoe store, and I could walk there instead of taking two buses each way to get to the mall where the shoe store was located. The hour or more saved in public transportation each way could be spent working more hours and earning more money. The time savings and increased income, coupled with the money saved not having to pay for the bus, was about equal to what I could earn in a good week selling candy. I ventured into a few other side sales deals to turn some quick profit, but those were short-lived. My desire to "get rich quick" increased proportionally to my decreasing satisfaction with my life at home and school. I was quickly spiraling into the terrible teens, and my mother saw the changes in me. My mother was always pretty good about letting me learn from my mistakes. I'm not really sure how much she knew or didn't know about my candy business or my growing desire to acquire as much cash as possible, but she had to know something was up.

It was about this time that my mother started opening up a lot more about her own job, and the jobs she worked in her youth. She worked while she was pregnant with me, and as soon after my birth as possible she returned to work. Not working was never an option for her, and I never felt like it was an option for me either. This is when my mother really started pushing me about the quality of work life I'd choose and how my work choices make me feel about myself. She reinforced that there is no such thing as a get rich quick scheme, and even if you do find something that seems easy and generates cash quickly, you need to do your research and make sure you fully understand what your business is all about. Is it legal? Is it ethical? Can you talk freely about your work and be proud of what you do, or do you behave in secretive ways? Do you wake up dreading going to work or in a hurry to get to work? Does the time you are at work seem to go on forever or move by quickly? She stressed that every day can't be a great day, and I'd likely need to have a few less than ideal jobs while preparing myself for the next better opportunity, but that my work must be honest.

She also reminded me that getting in trouble in school is not good, but it is better than ending up in jail. I hated working at Wendy's and worked with some shady people who were attempting to draw me into some lucrative but dangerous business propositions (the type of business that would be conducted out of the back of the store or in the trash hut behind the store). Oh the money was tempting, and the schemes always sounded so easy. If I had stayed at Wendy's, it would have eventually led to trouble, so I knew I needed to search for a new job. I pretty quickly found a nice and decent paying job with a market research and telemarketing firm. It was located right next to the train station one town over, and within a couple miles of my high school, so I could walk there or catch a bus (I was still too young to drive legally). I was able to work after school a few days a week until

9 or 10 pm, and on Saturdays, then catch the train home and still get my homework done. My mother was supportive, and made other after-school arrangements for my sister so I'd be free to work and still participate in the co-curricular activities I enjoyed.

The environment in which I grew up certainly had its impact on my sense of money, but also how it related to my sense of self-worth. When I was in the fifth grade, my family moved one town west, just a little closer to New York City, but into a wealthier area of the county. The elementary school I had attended through fourth grade was predominantly middle income, and I never recalled even being aware that my clothing had a brand. I always had my own style, and my mother would let me pick out my own clothes, but in fifth grade two things changed. First, I entered puberty. I was always really skinny, but overnight I chunked up. Second, I was starting a new school. Not a good combination.

My back to school shopping that year involved Husky Toughskins from Sears. My new peers made me instantly aware of how unsatisfactory I was. Some of them had never even heard of Sears, much less shopped there, and they would never actually wear anything that said "husky" on it. I might as well have embroidered "fat ass" across the seat of my jeans. Despite how tight money was, my mother understood that salvaging what little was left of my self esteem was truly a need at that moment, so we did our research and scraped up enough cash to upgrade me to a pair of Wranglers and a pair of Lees, which for the moment made me at least acceptable in school, though bought me no social status. Levi's would have been cooler, but the label showed your waist size, so I was willing to trade cool points to avoid announcing to the world the exact size of my girth.

Luckily, the summer between fifth and sixth grade, puberty continued its aggressive control of my hormones and physique, and all the good things grew in the right ways, and my waist shrunk. This was my second chance to make a good first impression, and we don't get too many of those. Through my fifth grade shame, I received a crash course in all things cool in this bold new world of Lakeside elementary school. The designer jean craze was just exploding, and show off the new slimmer me. It was time for back to ping, but the new wrinkle was that my sister was now _____ kindergarten, so she had back to school clothing needs as well. This would mean a little less cash for my clothes, and my dream of a designer wardrobe was out of the question. So the financial negotiations began.

I needed new clothes that would fit my new frame, but I wanted some designer jeans. My mother and I made a deal. We would shop for the essentials for my sister first, knowing those items would cost less, then I could have whatever was left from the back to school budget. How I chose to spend it was up to me. If I wanted one fancy designer outfit, I could have it, but I would be wearing it every day to school. With my smaller waist size I could now respectably wear a pair of Levi's, which cost less than the new designer brands, but still more than Wrangler. To stay in budget and have enough clothes to get me through the school week, I gave up the designer dream for the moment. But I did save whatever I could, and asked for cash for Christmas, and successfully returned from winter break in a pair of flea market Jordache jeans (I'm pretty sure they were authentic, well at least the label was authentic).

Once the clothes bug bit, and positive peer attention reinforced the better your labels the better you were, my desire for popular brands continued to grow. Unfortunately, as a result of my parents' divorce, our budget continued to diminish. My mother always kept her bargain and allowed me to make my own choices within budget. One summer I was playing bingo at the local Catholic church and won the big jackpot that night—$100. That was a fortune to me at the time, and in a gesture of gratitude for my mother's previous generosity and her difficult circumstances at that moment, I offered to budget my own back to school clothes that year from my winnings.

That is pretty much how things progressed for a few years. My mother provided what she could, I found ways to earn the rest, and we took advantage of opportunities to stretch our dollars however we could. Flea markets, outlets, tax free shopping with my grandmother in Pennsylvania (that is how I acquired my first Izod shirts), and making friends who wore the same size as me so we could borrow each other's clothing and make our peers think we had more than we really did.

Despite my best efforts, I made many mistakes along the way, and got myself into a bit of trouble. The lure of popularity and desire for nice clothes led me to the dangerous world of credit cards. Back in those days, department store credit cards were easy to acquire, and there was minimal if any information verification. My first credit card was from Gimbel's (they are no longer in business, but I'm pretty sure it wasn't my fault). I was 14 and on a whim filled out an application assuming it would get rejected. I indicated my date of birth was a bit earlier in the 60s than it actually is, and a few weeks later I get my first credit card. I didn't use it often, and would pay it off in full with cash in the store (I didn't have a checking account yet). Over the next year or so, feeling empowered by my success with Gimbel's, I applied for more department store cards. By the time I left for college, I had cards from JCPenney, Sterns, and Macy's. For a teenager I did a pretty good job managing credit cards I shouldn't have even had, but then there came the first month that I was short on cash and couldn't pay the full balance. Then came the interest, and the next month there still wasn't enough cash to cover the bill, and there came more interest. It took a long time to pay off those cards, but I always paid the minimum balance due so at least I wouldn't mess up my credit.

After I turned 18, I thought it would be best to cancel all those old credit cards and establish some new credit with my proper date of birth. Every now and then I would still get odd little reminders of my earlier deception. Shortly after turning 25 I received a letter from JCPenney offering me such a deal on life insurance. The letter read, "As you prepare for your thirties, your family needs are changing . . ." I just laughed. I guess that is what I get for advancing myself beyond the calendar. While I stopped lying on credit card applications, my tendency to "round up" when discussing my age continued. I considered it a necessary survival technique. People treat you very differently in college when they learn you are 16 years old, and the same was true in graduate school when I was 20. Being the only person in my graduate school cohort who couldn't legally drink was stressful, so it seemed easier to just let people assume how old I was, and I chose not to correct them.

Credit cards weren't the only area where I experienced a little financial trouble in my youth. My freshman year in college I ran out of money on my meal plan. The required meal plan was pretty basic, and everything was a la carte. There were great food choices on campus, including an ice cream shop, a sit down restaurant in an old train depot, and a pizza place. Where I really got into trouble was that the pizza place would deliver at night to your residence hall room and all you had to do was call in with your ID card number. My declining balance was quickly going down and my weight was quickly going up. I didn't even make it half way through the semester when my balance hit zero. Through my financial aid I had a federal work study job on campus, working the desk at the recreation center making $3.35 per hour for 20 hours per week. I was struggling to pay off old credit card debt and cover current expenses, and couldn't afford to purchase another meal plan. I broke down and called my mother. She heard my sob story, and said she would think about it and call me back with a decision.

Just like Ronald Reagan, my mother believed that you should "trust but verify," another trait I didn't appreciate at the time, but wish more parents believed in today. I could write an entire book on the inane accusations that parents make based on the assumption that everything their students tell them is Gospel. If I've heard it once I've heard it a thousand times, "my child would never lie to me." As Seth Meyers from Saturday Night Live would say, "Really?" Does any parent truly believe that? Have you not caught your kid with crumbs all over his mouth as he insists he didn't eat that cookie? If I weren't the professional college administrator that I am, I would say, "Give me a break. Who is a more credible source—your 18 year old who was caught with beer on campus or the hearing officer who has been lied to by hundreds of 18 year olds saying it wasn't their beer?" Common sense is not so common anymore.

One of my favorite experiences was dealing with the mother of a young man who flipped off and cursed at a campus police officer in front of the patrol car. The entire thing was captured on the patrol vehicle's video recording system. The student brought his mother to the hearing, and after I issued the student his sanction, the mother stood up and slammed her hands on the table, yelling at me that her son was innocent. I played the video for her, in which her son was easily identifiable and clearly engaged in the behaviors exactly as the officer described. My mother would never have attended such a hearing in the first place, but had she been there, this is the point when she would have slapped me in the back of the head and apologized to the college administrator for wasting his time and walked me over to the police officer to issue a full apology. But that was not the inclination of this mother. The woman with as serious an expression as I've ever seen insisted that I superimposed her son's face into that video and am attempting to frame him. Continuing a rational discussion becomes quite difficult at that point. I guess that apple didn't fall far from the tree. But I digress.

Upon verifying with the college that my meal plan truly was exhausted, and inquiring how exactly this had happened, my mother called me back to make a deal. She was willing to acknowledge that the standard meal plan was really not sufficient to last the entire semester, but also held me responsible for my poor meal plan management. She agreed to add some value to my card, but not to purchase a complete plan. She didn't want me to starve, but she didn't feel it was her responsibility to fund my late night pizzas, my ice cream snacks, or my train depot restaurant dates. She also made it clear that this was the only meal plan addition she was going to provide, so I'd better manage it more wisely. I barely made it to the end of the term, and luckily the spring semester came with a replenished meal plan.

I was more cautious the second semester, but still expended the full value of my meal plan by the first week of April and had about three weeks to go. I just didn't have the cash to replenish my meal plan for the final few weeks, so I swallowed my pride, said a little prayer, and called my mother. No need for contemplation or a call back this time. Mom's response was simple and direct: no. I tried playing the guilt card and asked how I was supposed to stay alive if I had no money for food. I'll never forget my mother's response:

"I have enough faith that you are smart enough not to let yourself starve."

At first I thought she was playing hardball and I just needed to beg. No dice. She was emphatic. She asked me, "Was I unclear when I told you last fall that I wouldn't put any more money on your meal plan?"

Nope—she was pretty clear.

I pressed anyway. "Fine, you're right, can I just have a little loan then?" Strong and firm as an oak tree, my mother did not waiver. I was pissed.

As I reiterated this unbelievable story to my roommate, my friends, the person I was dating, I grew angrier and said some not-so-nice things about my mother. Naturally my fellow college students agreed with me and couldn't believe my mother was so unreasonable and uncaring. At the end of my financial rope, I relied on the generosity of friends to get me through until my next paycheck, and made some meals out of snack machines. Once I got paid, I went shopping and bought two boxes of ziti, some generic tomato sauce, a block of mozzarella cheese, and a two pack of disposable aluminum trays. Baked ziti was cheap, easy to make, and easy to reheat. I couldn't really afford meat anyway, but by leaving the meat out I figured the dish would last longer.

Those two trays of baked ziti got me through the rest of the semester. On the days when I really couldn't stand eating another serving of baked ziti, I would go to Everybody's restaurant on the edge of Emory's campus and get a side salad. Everybody's would let you sit as long as you wanted, so I brought my homework. The side salad was only a couple bucks, but was pretty large and had lots of good stuff in it that wasn't in my baked ziti. Everybody's also gave you unlimited crackers on the table, so I'd sit for hours and nurse my salad while eating every last pack of crackers on the table, and then requested a refill. A full basket of crackers would arrive in time for me to finish my salad, get the check, and when the waitress would walk away I'd stash the entire basket of crackers in my backpack for a snack the next day.

My mother was absolutely right. I was smart enough to survive, and by denying my request she gave me one of her best gifts ever.

She could have given me a fish and I would have had a meal for a day, but instead she forced me to go fishing and I learned to feed myself forever.

Years later I did eventually thank my mother for being so strong and not giving in. I figured that was the best way I could return her gift, by validating her wisdom. She started to break down a little and confided how difficult a decision it was for her. I always assumed she was just doing what she thought was right and it had no real impact on her. I was wrong. She shared how she cried when she hung up the phone because she wanted to just give me the money, but knew it was not what I really needed. She didn't want me to have to rely on anyone but myself, and needed me to know I could take care of my own problems. At that moment I finally understood what it meant when a parent would say "this is going to hurt me more than it is going to hurt you," before spanking a child. Doing the right thing can be painful, but out of that conflict comes critical growth (thanks again, Kohlberg—re-read the Preface if you missed this reference).

I think the greatest lesson my mother taught me in the realm of money relates to making personal choices and taking responsibility. She started teaching me this lesson long before the meal plan incident in college. Telling a kid that making certain mistakes will cost you money in your adulthood tends to fall on deaf ears. Start charging the kid when he makes mistakes and he gets the message loud and clear. It didn't take long for my mother to realize that "normal" punishments didn't work on me. Especially after the divorce, the threat of "wait until your father gets home" was gone. Since I hit puberty early, I was taller and physically stronger than my mother by the end of elementary school. Threatening a smack or digging her fingernails into the underside of my arm quickly lost its effectiveness. She could try punishing me, but I wasn't listening. I'd wait until she went to sleep and sneak out of my bedroom window, which was in the basement and easy to navigate. What is a struggling single mother to do with an obnoxious adolescent? Hit your kid where it really hurts—the wallet!

My mother knew I understood the value of a dollar and the importance of having sufficient means to cover life's essential needs and desires; after all, she had taught me those lessons throughout my childhood. She created the perfect punishment for me—a fee scale. What happens when you pay a bill late, or fail to submit a necessary document, or cause damage? It costs you money. I knew her pay days because that is when we received our allowance, so she took the concept of allowance one step further. The same way completing my chores and contributing to the household earned me money, breaking household rules would cost me money. The choice was mine.

Having a good time with friends, but curfew is upon you? Is being thirty minutes late worth $5? Maybe, maybe not, but how many times could I afford to do that before my allowance was gone and I owed my mother money? Cursing, being disrespectful, not calling when I was told to, not being where I said I would be, all had its price. It was an amazingly effective strategy with me. What good was it to hang out with my friends if I didn't have enough money to do anything? What if I owed my mother on payday and I refused to pay? She had lots of options. Deduct the debt from my savings account or college fund, cut off my access to certain household privileges like laundry or charge for use of those services, not buy any food I would enjoy, not let me join the rest of the family for a family outing or meal out, ask me not to eat with the rest of the family or ignore me if I refuse to leave the dining room . . . oh the possibilities were endless.

These embargos were typically effective, but there were some times when even economic sanctions were not sufficient. My mother knew there was no use trying to diminish my desire for freedom, so instead she reinforced my freedom of choice, but made sure I knew the potential consequences for those choices, and that she was willing to do what was necessary to enforce the consequences. If internal reinforcement didn't work, my mother made sure I understood she would involve outside resources. My mother would never want to call the police on me, but I know she would do it if she needed to or if it was truly what I needed to learn an important lesson (and when it was necessary she did indeed involve the police). When she made a promise, she kept it. I didn't like it, but I respected it. And at the end of the day, isn't it more important that kids respect their parents than that they like them?

As adults, my mother and I are now great friends having recreated our relationship as responsible independent people who choose to engage each other because we genuinely enjoy each other, but it was not her job to be my friend . . . it was her job to be my parent. And she took her job seriously and did it well.

# CHAPTER 4

# CHOICES AND RESPONSIBILITY

Many of the themes of this book overlap, and in the Venn diagram of life lessons, choices and responsibilities, or choices and consequences, fall in the middle. If there was a singular most important category of life lessons it was likely this one. The particular sect of Judeo-Christian belief under which I was raised, coupled with American democratic ideology, focused at the foundation upon freedom of personal choice. A little Calvinist predetermination would slip in from time to time, particularly in difficult times when it was easier to believe "everything happens for a reason and we must trust in God's plan." However, we were not people to rely on predestination as an excuse to diminish personal choice and responsibility. I have to admit I struggled, especially as a kid, with the concept of omniscience. How can I truly be free to make whatever choices I wish if God already knows the choices I'm going to make and the subsequent consequences of those choices? The logic didn't work for me.

My mother did a better job of explaining it than the church. Her first approach to satisfying an overly inquisitive kid was to hope I would just accept the basic explanation that God knows the choices we are going to make, but we still get to make them. Over time the explanations shifted more into an intuition and pattern response approach, but none the less, the clear message I received from very early on is that I am free to do whatever I want any time I want, but I'm also free to suffer the consequences. It was much easier to get me on board with a behavioral plan if I was involved in the decision making, rather than dictate to me what I can and cannot do.

"So this means I can jump off the roof?"

"Sure, you are physically capable of jumping off the roof, but you'll likely die or minimally get really badly hurt, and then you won't be able to walk or do the many other things you enjoy doing in life. So, temping as it seems to jump off the roof, is it worth it?"

"No, I guess the risk is too great, so the right choice is not to jump off the roof."

Despite the arguments that kids do not have the capacity to reason, even young children are far more in touch with their environment than we sometimes give them credit. I learned this from some incredibly insightful remarks my niece had made to me when she was four years old during a visit. She was commenting on a disagreement her parents were having, and had previously had on more than one occasion, based on what she had ascertained simply being within earshot of them. Even when we think they aren't listening, children are always listening. Of course this may vary from child to child, and there may be limits to the level of engaged reasoning with very small children, but when I do get the opportunity to speak with kids, even very young ones, they continue to amaze me with their intuitive natures. But this chapter is not about child development, the breadth and depth of human reasoning, or theological perspectives. It will be much more fun than that, I promise!

Let's start with the house fire. First off, I blame my mother. It's her fault for teaching me to be so conscientious about the value of money and the effort involved in earning it. It was fall and I was in the seventh grade. One of my chores was raking the leaves. We had a pretty large yard and lots of trees, thus lots of leaves. I did my best to negotiate a per bag rate since I thought that would generate a larger yield for me. My mother, fearing I would under stuff the bags to increase the bag count, and in doing so increase the number of pricey lawn bags we'd need to purchase, held firm on a flat rate for the job. Despite my best negotiating efforts, my mother's mind could not be changed, and I was left to accept the terms of her deal. Not wanting to spend more time or effort than necessary since it would diminish my profit margin, I thought the best approach was to gather the leaves, burn them, and have far less material to bag. I found a friend willing to help for almost nothing, so I thought I had my mother beat.

The stage is set, and my friend is scheduled to meet me after school so we can knock the job out long before my mother gets home and finds out I solicited assistance. We worked quickly and got the leaves raked onto the driveway in a huge pile so we could set the fire and not burn the grass. I got the extra long matches that we used to light the fireplace, and a bucket of sand to make sure the fire was fully extinguished before bagging the remains. I was so proud of myself and couldn't believe how smart I was. I duped a friend into providing nearly free labor, I was knocking out a huge job that could have taken me many more hours to accomplish on my own using the more traditional rake and bag method. That was a fool's approach and I was no fool.

I struck the first match, holding it low to the ground, trying to ignite a small cluster of leaves. Minor charring at best, but no flames emerged. I struck the second match and tried again. Strike two. Maybe the wind was the problem. So I tried another section of the pile, a bit closer to the house, where the wind was blocked more. Strike three. In baseball I would be out.

Knowing the definition of insanity is doing the same thing over and over again and expecting a different result, I figured I needed a different approach. When trying to light the coals in the grill, some lighter fluid helps. So I headed down to the basement on a quest for lighter fluid. Time was ticking, no lighter fluid in sight, and the wind was picking up. If we have to re-rake all those leaves, that would ruin my entire plan. Time for creative thinking . . . hmmm, what burns quick? Vodka! Alcohol burns, and I know where the vodka is (truth be told I'd snuck a little sip from time to time, and nobody seemed to notice, so a shot or two to fuel the fire shouldn't be missed).

Back outside on the driveway, vodka in hand, I sprinkled a little on a section of leaves. Doesn't look wet enough, maybe just a little more. The wind had indeed picked up a bit, so I stood under the edge of the carport, and started with the leaves closest to the carport, hoping the wind would not diminish my efforts. I struck the match and placed the flame into the section of vodka-soaked leaves closest to me. Boy that vodka is flammable! That section of leaves quickly flamed up, emitting what felt like a thousand degree flash of heat with flames dancing ten feet into the air.

My friend and I jumped back, caught completely off guard, and I fell into one of the plastic garbage cans leaning against the house under the carport. In doing so, the first garbage can bumped the second garbage can, which ricocheted off the house in a manner that appeared physically impossible, landing into the pile of leaves right where the fire was spreading. My head was spinning and everything was simultaneously moving really quickly and really slowly. Doing my best to compose myself, I felt momentarily paralyzed as the garbage can began to engulf in flames growing ever upward, tickling the corrugated Lucite that covered the carport so precariously attached to the house on one side and secured by wooden posts into the ground just beyond the driveway on the other.

As the flames continued to grow and spread, throughout the pile of leaves, fully engulfing both garbage cans, dancing along the inner covering of the carport and snaking around the wooden posts, I felt a strong hand grab my shoulder and pull me back. It was the neighbor from across the street. He was a tall, strong, silent man, maybe in his mid-50s at the time. He never really spoke to me, and I found him both odd and scary. His wife was also a bit odd, but much more pleasant. Despite my predicament, he was the last person I wanted to see.

He attempted to turn on the exterior faucet near the side door, but my grandfather, always one to be prepared, had already winterized the house and turned off all exterior water sources from inside the basement. There wasn't time to re-engage an exterior water source and find a hose. In one of the most amazing moves I've ever seen, this intimidating, immense, and rigid man, who seemed incredibly old to me at the time, leapt in the most singular and graceful way over the three foot fence that separated my yard from the next door neighbors'. Luckily the neighbors had not yet winterized (I'm not sure if everyone on the block did that kind of thing), and still had a hose lying alongside their house. The across the street neighbor grabbed the hose of the next door neighbor and began dousing the carport and side of the house, then focused on the base of the fire.

Single-handedly my neighbor extinguished the fire, returned the hose to its rightful owner, and provided guidance on how best to tackle the most immediate remediation. My mother's imminent arrival was growing nigh, and in the most stoic yet sympathetic manner my neighbor suggested that my friend return to his own home, and that I attend to my immediate business while he and his wife await the arrival of my mother. Broom in hand, I began sweeping the wet ashes in the driveway, hoping that by some miracle I could diminish the alarming view of this scene before my mother's first encounter.

It wasn't long before I heard the distinctive sound of my mother's Subaru turbo engine approaching, and then suddenly the rumbling diminished and the air was eerily calm and quiet. I peered around the corner of the house, and there in the middle of the street, just far enough away from the driveway that my mother had no visual connection with the carport that momentarily became a pyre, I saw the neighbors standing alongside the passenger door of my mother's car.

After what seemed an eternity, I saw the neighbors retreat toward their home, my mother's window raise, and her car slowly progress toward and then into the driveway. I stepped into the middle of the driveway, far enough in front of the rubble to prevent her from advancing her vehicle into it. Clearly I had lost my mind, and luckily my mother didn't lose hers. In retrospect, I'm sure the temptation to just run me down in the driveway was overwhelming, and I do recall thinking that the car appeared to be accelerating as she approached. From outside the vehicle I could almost feel my mother slam on the breaks within less than a foot from where I was standing, and the heat from the front grill upon my legs was immediately reminiscent of the blaze from such a short time prior.

Before my mother could even exit the car, I walked to the driver's side door and blurted out "I'm so sorry, but I'm OK." I received "the look" that said everything without my mother needing to utter a word as she exited the vehicle and walked past me to enter the side door of the house. As she opened the storm door, without even looking back at me, she said a bit too calmly, "you WILL fix this." And then she simply retreated to her bedroom.

When we finally did discuss the situation, I, like a young adolescent is wont to do, attempted to provide excuses and rationalizations that would somehow diminish my culpability. My mother was having none of this. My mother firmly inquired if I had any capacity or capability to turn back the hands of time and undo what has been done. Of course I had to concede that I did not.

"So what are your options? Nobody can go backwards, so why waste the energy to stress about the past. It is what it is. Put your energy into the future, fixing what is wrong, and preventing yourself from making the same foolish choices again."

Sure she was mad, and there is a lot she could have said and done. But to what end? My mother did later share that the neighbors were a tremendous help. At the side of her car the night of the fire, they first assured her everyone was fine, but explained that there was an accident, but it wasn't as bad as it could have been, and everything can be repaired. Had my mother happened upon the damage without neighborly forewarning, the immediate response may have been different, but the end result would not.

As our discussion of post-fire restoration ensued, my mother set very clear expectations. First, I would provide all the funding myself for the materials necessary to fully repair all the damage. Second, I would provide the labor, at no charge. I could understand and accept the first provision, but cautiously objected to the second. I was the "brains" of the family, but had little to no inclination for this type of handiwork. Couldn't I just pay for someone else to do it? She was clear and firm: "No."

Since I made what appeared to be the easy choice and attempted to bypass my initial responsibility and agreement for appropriately disposing of the leaves, it was now my responsibility to fully rectify the situation myself. Despite the various lessons my mother taught me about money management, she also taught me that money cannot solve every problem. There are things in life you must do yourself, by yourself, or for yourself. And this was one of them.

I mildly protested, "So how am I supposed to figure out how to fix all this stuff?"

My mother solicited the assistance of my grandfather, who was very skilled in a variety of trades, and he was to serve as my foreman, supervising the entire project. Luckily we lived in a solid brick house, so the primary structure itself sustained little damage beyond the window frames and screens, and lots of soot. Winter came quickly that year, so full restoration would not be completed until the following summer, when I would learn how to scrape, sand, paint, string and install screens, etc. My grandfather had very high standards, so I knew to do things correctly the first time, because he would not hesitate to make me do it again if he wasn't satisfied. The perfectionist gene definitely runs strong in my family.

I learned a lot of lessons that year, many stemming from the infamous fire. Some things in life just need to be done certain ways, and sometimes those ways are difficult. There is nothing wrong with being creative and trying to build a better mousetrap, but thorough research and testing is needed before execution. When things don't go as planned, take responsibility for the consequences and whatever is necessary for resolution. Don't stress about the past because nobody can change it; invest your energy in the future, fixing the problems and preventing reoccurrence. Part of problem resolution may be financial, but money alone cannot fix everything. A number of situations would reinforce these lessons for me throughout my young adulthood.

After the fire, another major moment of crisis that would reinforce the lessons of choice and responsibility for me was the summer between tenth and eleventh grades. I was in one of my first "serious" relationships, and I made the choice to become sexually active. I thought my girlfriend was on the pill, and didn't feel the need to take any further level of protection. This was very early into the AIDS crisis and our knowledge of safer sex was incredibly limited, as were our assumptions of who was at risk and what activities were in the clear. This was also an incredibly naïve time in my personal romantic development, assuming lust equaled love, and people could be trusted at face value.

My girlfriend informed me that she missed her period and was pretty sure she was pregnant. I inquired how that could be possible if she was on the pill. She responded, "Oh, I was having problems with that, so I stopped taking it."

This was critical information that would have been useful to know about two months earlier. My girlfriend was very cavalier about the whole thing, and didn't seem to understand why I was upset. I quickly moved beyond my confusion and anger, and reoriented myself into a posture of love. Maybe this was a blessing in disguise. I wasn't ready to start a family, but maybe this was a sign that this is the girl I'm meant to marry and spend my life with, and her going off the pill was divine intervention. I started creating a fantasy in my mind of this perfect life. That fantasy was quickly shattered.

I went home that evening and my mother was already asleep. I have no idea why I felt compelled to wake her up and tell her the news at that very moment, but as if I were hovering above my own body, I watched myself head straight to my mother's bedroom door and knock ever so lightly. No response. A bit more forcefully, the second knock caused a rumbling from inside, and I was invited to enter. Without turning on the light, having just the illumination from the hallway behind me to create a minimal glow of recognition, I could make out my mother's face, though I'm pretty sure she could not clearly see mine. I hesitated a moment, then began to speak in stuttering tones that were not characteristic of my normal communication. My mother, tired and appearing to grow somewhat frustrated, finally said, "What's wrong?"

I told her my girlfriend was pregnant. She asked if I was the father.

How insulting! Who else would be the father?

My mother's question was foreshadowing another important life lesson she would teach me. Sometimes people lie, either directly or by omission, and my mother's intuition about my girlfriend's character was far superior to my own. I made the mistake of investing more faith in a young girl from another town who I had known less than a year, and really spent very little time with, over my mother who had known me my entire life and who was far more invested in my happiness and well-being. Good luck trying to explain that to a horny teenager!

I'm sure my mother sensed my hurt and disbelief in this line of questioning, and she quickly dropped it and asked what I planned to do. I began regaling her with dreams of the perfect life with the white picket fence in the suburbs and what a perfect father I would be, not making the mistakes that my parents made.

My wise mother, even in her slumbered state, realized I was momentarily unreachable as I swooned in the stratosphere. She suggested we speak the next day. Oh and we did.

The next morning, before I had a chance to launch into delusion again, my mother sat me down and made a few choice statements. My mother said, "First, if you are the father then this is your responsibility and you WILL completely fulfill your responsibility. That means more than just monetary child support. Being a father means being present and engaged in raising the child, and accepting that parenthood is a lifelong job."

She continued to offer additional points, and while these may not have been her exact words, I vividly remember the core content of her message.

She continued, "Second, fulfilling your responsibility does NOT necessarily mean marriage. Marriage for the wrong reasons could result in divorce; don't make a decision that appears wise in the short-run if the long-term consequences are highly likely to be disastrous."

Without true love ("adult" love, not "kid" love) and mutual devotion, respect and commitment, a marriage will likely not survive, or minimally be problematic and stressful.

Her third and most important point was that parenthood is hard and changes your entire life. "Dreams of college, parties, nice clothes, hobbies, disposable income, may all have to be postponed, sometimes indefinitely, when the responsibilities of parenthood happen upon you too soon. But, you made the choice to have sex and you made the choice to trust that your girlfriend was on the pill, and you made the choice to not provide yourself with any additional protection both against pregnancy and possible disease. These were all within your control, and based on the choices you made, you will now have to contemplate the consequences and fulfill the responsibilities. The choices you made at that one instant have now dictated future choices you will make for a lifetime."

My mother understood these things well since she had lived them. She sacrificed her dreams of a college education because of me. She was a straight A student with a promising future, just like me. My bubble had burst.

Later that day, my girlfriend and I spoke and I told her that I shared the news with my mother. My girlfriend grew angry and questioned why I would do that. How could I not? My mother may have burst my bubble, but my girlfriend decimated it.

"I haven't even decided what I'm doing yet, so how could you tell your mother?"

"I'm confused, what does this mean?"

"Maybe I'll just get an abortion."

I hadn't even considered that possibility. I knew girls in school who had gotten them, but I never really thought about it personally. My girlfriend was Jewish, and in her interpretation of Judaism everything is about the maternal line, which she extrapolated to mean everything was about what she wanted. I was certainly no expert in Judaism, but I had enough exposure through my own Jewish relatives and my many, many Jewish friends and classmates to question her interpretations. I had also learned some lessons from a Passover incident at her house earlier that spring, but I'll share that story later.

I tried to argue for what I perceived were my rights, but that argument seemed to fall on deaf ears, even with my mother. As she explained, it is difficult to compare the minimal level of investment I had made at that point in a few unintentional and awkward moments compared to the level of investment the young woman would have to make in carrying the child to term, even if she were willing to give the child over to me. I felt powerless. Was I being selfish wanting to keep the baby? Wouldn't life be easier for all of us if she just had an abortion? Was my future really indelibly linked and controlled by a singular decision made by this one girl?

The week continued, and still no period. My girlfriend took numerous home pregnancy tests, and claimed they were all positive. I never actually saw the results of any of them. She was adamant that her family not know anything, and asked me to swear my mother to secrecy. My mother never made a promise she didn't feel she could keep, so she simply said she would do what she believed was right based on the circumstances of this situation as it unfolded. And goodness did this situation unfold!

Later that week my girlfriend informed me that she went to see her doctor, who assured her he would keep her secret from her parents (would a family doctor really do that with a minor?). During that visit the doctor allegedly confirmed her pregnancy, and told her when she conceived and when she was due. Either my girlfriend had a bad memory, or thought I was an idiot, or was trying to give me a message without having to come out and tell me something, but the date the conception supposedly occurred was during a week when I was out of town. For a really smart guy, sometimes I was a little slow on the uptake. Once I put two and two together, I naturally assumed the doctor was wrong. She couldn't have gotten pregnant during the week he claimed because we hadn't had sex that week.

By the time my girlfriend and I were together again face to face, and I had the opportunity to inquire about this discrepancy in the calendar, I could see the disappointing truth in her face. I wasn't the father. Evidently while I was out of town on a family camping trip, my girlfriend became bored and lonely and decided to hang out with her ex-boyfriend, with whom she was still very friendly. She told me that even though they knew they couldn't be together, they would always love each other, and since a woman never really gets over her first love, I couldn't blame her for her momentary lapse in judgment. She also shared that she spoke with her ex-boyfriend about this and he wanted nothing to do with the baby, and had no desire to get between she and I. In an interesting twist, my girlfriend now expressed how she could never abort this baby, especially now knowing who the biological father was. She knew he would never marry her or help her raise the baby, but she knew I was a good and honorable person, and since we were together and in love, it didn't matter how she got pregnant, all that mattered was raising the child in a loving and stable home. She said her pregnancy was kismet and we needed to fulfill our destinies and get married and raise the child.

Among my many virtues and dysfunctions, one of the greatest among them is my sense of duty. Much like Frederic in *Pirates of Penzance*, I can allow my function to become my folly, and this situation was a case in point. I allowed my "need to be needed" to supersede my common sense, and agreed to "do the right thing" and make an honorable woman of my girlfriend and raise a family together, keeping her secret about the true identity of the child's biological father. I guess in some twisted way I thought of myself like Joseph, having fatherhood thrust upon me for some greater good, and despite my lack of biological responsibility, this young woman needed me and I should not reject her. Of course there was nothing miraculous or divine about this conception, and I was just fooling myself. I made a valiant effort to suppress the truth from everyone, including my mother. After all, my pride was on the line.

Since my mother's first question when I told her about the pregnancy was "are you the father?" she obviously sensed something I could not, and how could I possibly admit to her that she was right? The whole situation was eating me up inside, and I was growing more conflicted. I wanted to honor my promise to my girlfriend to marry her, but I knew we were too young to get legally married and I didn't think my mother would sign the necessary papers. I had to tell her the truth, and trust that she would know what I should do.

My mother never ceases to amaze and impress me. I prepared myself for "I told you so" and "you damn fool, you need to break up with her right now." Instead, I was greeted with compassion and understanding. My mother assured me of how honorable my intentions were, and gently led me to also see how misguided they were. However, my mother never attempted to make the decision for me. The choice would be mine. If I really was in love with this girl, and I really believed this was the best course of action for my life, my mother would provide her blessing. The responsibilities of my choice would also remain fully mine.

As circumstance would have it, the decision was made for us. A couple of weeks later, I attempted to have sex with my girlfriend, and she grew defensive and said she was on her period and couldn't have sex. Thoroughly confused, I inquired how she was having a period if she was pregnant? She said she had some bad cramping during that week, which was followed by some spotting. She went to her doctor and he said she lost the baby, but she was too upset and ashamed to discuss it with me.

The icing on the cake was that she supposedly discussed it with her ex-boyfriend, since after all, he was the father. So in other words, I'm just the schmuck she intended to use to pay for the mistake they made. I needed air. I walked out of her house and all the way home. I was too young to drive, and didn't want to ask her parents for a ride or call my mother, so I just walked the approximately nine miles home for what seemed like hours. I cried, I yelled, I cursed, and I was downright confused as hell.

Was she ever really pregnant? Was I being manipulated as part of some elaborate ruse to make her ex-boyfriend jealous? We ended up not speaking for a while, and when we did, she would never give me any direct answers. We still saw each other from time to time, and we never had a formal moment of confrontation and break-up, our relationship just sort of faded away. To this day, I still don't know the truth.

Our concepts of truth are dependent upon the information available to us at any given moment. We trust that the sources of this information are accurate. Based upon what we believe to be true, we make our choices in life, and calculate the circumstances and responsibilities based upon these assumptions of truth. Faulty information, be it intentionally or unintentionally so, can lead us to make improperly informed choices that can result in unintended consequences. These consequences will not necessarily be negative, but it doesn't matter. Misinformation diminishes our ability to make accurate choices and to accurately assess potential consequences.

Why didn't my mother just tell me that my girlfriend was a liar and a slut? Evidently she had figured it out before I did? I had to know. If my mother was supposed to protect me, why didn't she just tell me what she thought? She replied, "Would you have believed me had I told you?"

She taught me another critical lesson that day. People will often seek your advice, and you are free to tell people exactly what you think, but if you tell them things they don't want to hear or aren't ready to acknowledge, they may misplace their anger, and you may become the target of their confusion or displeasure. If people are pleased with your advice, and choose to follow it, but things do not turn out as planned, then you may become the scapegoat. Either way, positive or negative, you run the substantial risk that the person seeking your advice may make their problem your problem, and now because of your choice to dispense your opinion, you may be assuming some of the responsibility for the consequences. My mother felt it was wiser to help guide me to reach my own conclusions, and empower me to make my own choices since I was ultimately the one who needed to live with the consequences.

To this day, my mother will share her perspectives, but in a balanced way, that challenges you to consider every angle of the situation for yourself. Ultimately, the decision is yours.

I've adopted this same philosophy, or at least done my best to do so. I've learned that people find this frustrating. Most people would rather seek advice and have someone else tell them what to do. It is much easier, isn't it? Especially those of us who think we know best, why wouldn't people want to do as we tell them? I live with this challenge on a daily basis.

Every day I encounter students, and sometimes staff members, who want me to tell them what to do, and often how to do it. And to be honest, sometimes it is easier that way for me, too. I feel fairly confident in my abilities to make sound decisions and I feel pretty competent in doing my job and managing life's various tasks. Most Baby Boomers with whom I interact, and many Gen Xers, feel the same. The Millennials, not so much.

Daily I encounter many people who seek specific instructions on how life is to be lived, and I struggle with the awesome responsibility of my profession. So many of these young people are great at following instructions, and have been raised by very involved and attentive parents with the best of intentions. The challenge is that many of these parents have instructed their children but not taught them. They have given their children safety and security and sheltered them from the difficulties of life, but not prepared them to think for themselves and make their own choices. These same parents remain highly involved in their children's lives well into adulthood, continuing to enable their children's inability to function independently.

If the "adults" continue to instruct the "children" without teaching them anything of substance and independence in the process, how will the next generation possibly assume its rightful place at the helm of society when the preceding generation passes? Is this not the crisis of leadership we hear so frequently discussed, and the crippling fear that our society hovers on the precipice of disaster? I'm not nearly that pessimistic, but I have a healthy concern. Part of my responsibility, well at least my choice, is to do my part to prepare young adults today for the roles they will play in the future to hopefully lead and improve our world, despite the unintended and often unrecognized efforts of their parents to the contrary.

One last reflection I'd like to share on choice and responsibility, but not a lesson from my childhood. This one is a reflection from my adulthood, though still a lesson I learned from my mother. Well, more accurately a lesson I learned from my grandfather, but vicariously through my mother. As we all do at family gatherings, old stories emerge, sometimes with new twists, and we wax and wane nostalgic. On just such an occasion, my mother was regaling company with the many misbehaviors of my childhood, which luckily are quite comical in retrospective. Then she segued into reflections on how these memories have become comical anecdotes, with the pain and struggle fully subsided, but at the time of their occurrence some of these situations seemed insurmountable. She shared intimate details of a conversation she had had with my grandfather during my particularly difficult years, around the time of the great fire.

As a single mother with a young daughter's welfare to consider, many of my adolescent shenanigans were taking a quick toll on my mother's sense of ability to maintain control and composure. I had often heard the threats to ship me away to a military academy, but given my family's limited means I assumed it was all just a bunch of hot air. Evidently I was wrong. At one point my mother had reached the conclusion that she could handle me no more, and the time had come to ship me off. She approached my grandfather to discuss options and resources. She expected him to be understanding and supportive, and hopefully help brainstorm ways to make it cost feasible. Much to her chagrin, this was not his response.

He simply asked her a poignant reflective question: "So the lesson you want to teach your son is that when his responsibilities become too difficult to manage, he should make his problems someone else's problems?"

That was all he needed to say. My mother had always lived by principles of responsibility, and taught those principles to her children in word and deed. How could she change her game plan now? What could be the long-term ramifications of taking the route that seemed easier at that moment?

I never ended up in a military academic, and maybe had I been sent off it would have given me some beneficial structure that could have enhanced my life in unknown ways. Maybe it would have stifled my creativity and ingenuity, and diminished my capacity for independence. Maybe I would have rebelled and been expelled, or minimally had the crap beaten out of me. We'll never know, but the result of my mother's choice not to send me away is known. She remained true to her principles, and continued to exhibit tremendous strength, courage, and wisdom as she made the difficult choice to fulfill her responsibilities, working through the conflicts and forcing all of us to grow in the process.

# CHAPTER 5

# OPTIMISM AND FORGIVENESS

My mother has lived a life full of difficulty and pain. Those are her stories to tell, but suffice it for me to share that the things I know of her difficulty and pain are primarily from my own observations, from second hand stories shared by other family members, or from comical reflections she has made during our adult interactions. As children, my mother did her best to avoid instilling guilt or pity in me and my sister. Even when I tried reaching out in support, my mother would do all in her power to absorb and resolve her own burdens. As previous chapters have described, we understood difficulty. My mother's approach was never to unrealistically shelter us from life, but she never wanted to unduly burden us with her own challenges either. Likewise, she had no tolerance for self-pity.

Everyone deserves the right to grieve after experiencing a loss, but the never-ending pity party or people who just thrive on drama, are unacceptable. If we ever felt a little too sorry for ourselves, my mother had no problem giving us a reality check and helping us understand what real suffering was all about. That could be done through awareness of world affairs or local community service, but it was important to have perspective and know there are always people with greater problems than your own.

Even in her greatest moments of angst, my mother has a tremendous capacity for optimism. Every cloud has a silver lining, and sometimes if you have difficulty seeing it, you just need to adjust your viewpoint. This optimism, coupled with what I consider a healthy and witty sense of humor, makes my mother one of the most pleasant people to be around. I add the caveat on her wit and humor because I share her talent in those arenas, but have been told by some that I'm more quirky than humorous, and I know she has heard the same retorts. I'm proud of this shared characteristic and am happy to receive the jabs, since I consider them a compliment to my mother.

There were some very messy moments during my parents' divorce. I was old enough to know what was going on, and have very vivid memories of some pretty horrible encounters between them. It is not my place to judge, nor air the family's dirty laundry, but I want it to be clear that I knew exactly what was going on and who did what and to whom. Despite what I knew or speculated that I knew, my mother always remained minimally neutral (if not positive) and respectful regarding my father, and her expectations for how we as children should treat him, or really anyone for that matter. Many of my friends and classmates were products of divorce and remarriage. In fact, by high school, it was odd to meet someone whose parents were still married to each other. Stories of messy divorces, hateful parents and grandparents, and various family unit mutations of steps and halves, were common lunchroom conversation.

My mother genuinely did her best to contain any quarrels with my father, and let us develop our own independent relationships with him (and his new wife and children), deciding for ourselves how we would feel about and respond to any corresponding actions or lack thereof. My sister, being just a small child and "Daddy's little girl" during the divorce, idolized my father and blamed my mother for "sending him away." Even when she would say insensitive things, and I was tempted to intervene, my mother would stop me and remind me that she didn't understand and she was just lashing out in pain. She needed to maintain a perfect image of her father and their unique relationship, and experience the stages of loss for how that relationship was changing.

I had a front row seat to my mother's single life, her dating, and eventual remarriage. Sometimes I was a silent observer (at least initially), but more often I perceived that it was my job to assess and filter, all the while maintaining my role of authority as Alpha male in the household. Add puberty to the mix and you've got a recipe for difficulty. My mother was patient and continued to take the high road. When she first started dating my stepfather, we all got along very well. He is a great cook, and I'm talking real meals with a variety of course options. Cooking was never really my mother's thing, and as soon as I was able I pretty much handled preparing the meals. What we considered meals were things like beanie wienies, fish sticks and fries, a baked chicken with a canned veggie side, steak ums, mac and cheese and spam, and of course regular fast food nights when we had nursing home or church commitments. Weekly traditions included KFC, pizza, and don't even get me started on the too rarely offered delicacy that is McDonald's McRib! Along came someone who introduced our hibernating palates to filet mignon, lobster tail, bisque, fresh vegetables, and other sundry casseroles.

Dating was fine, but marriage was another story. I didn't take the news of my mother's engagement well. I expressed my dissatisfaction in a variety of interesting ways. The height of these efforts was exhibited during the wedding reception. I wanted to do something to show everyone my love for my mother, so I decided to sing a song. Naturally my mother assumed it would be some lovely tribute to her new chapter in life and the love she shared with her new husband. Well wouldn't that be boring!

I had the perfect song. Helen Reddy's "You and Me Against the World."

My mother used to sing it to me as a young child, so how fitting that I should return the favor. To add insult to injury, I got myself drunk before the moment of my big debut. I'm not talking tipsy, I'm talking drunk. I was 15 years old at the time, and started downing vodka Collins at the reception before the bridal party even arrived. My otherwise melodious voice, from what others who were there tell me, left quite a lot to be desired. I keep hearing in my head the tune to "What do you do with a drunken sailor" but with the words, "what do you do with a drunken bride's son." Not one of my finer moments.

After the reception, I sensed my mother's frustration with me, so I thought it best to make myself useful. I decided to help load the wedding gifts into the car, which involved carrying them down a long narrow staircase. My mother asked me not to, and forewarned that in my condition I was likely to drop and break something since so many of the gifts were delicate. As usual, my mother's prediction came true, and I broke a rather pricey Lenox picture frame. My mother remained calm, and simply said, "You'll be buying us a new one." And I did.

These were the years that I could coin "hate the sin, but love the sinner." Almost anything you can imagine that a kid could do to upset a parent, I did. I always suffered the consequences, but I was also always forgiven. Nobody has ever embodied grace for me like my mother. When enough was finally enough with my negative attitude toward her new marriage, she sat me down and made her perspective crystal clear.

"You are my son and I will always love you as my son, but this is not about you. This is about me. The day will come, and pretty soon, when you will go off to college and start your own life, and eventually your sister will move on. What would you wish for me? To be alone and miserable? This is my husband and you have two choices—like it or don't, but either way, for your own good, get over it. This will be the last time we discuss this."

And it was. And I did, get over it, and chose to like him, and grew to love him. After I left for college I really came to appreciate everything my stepfather provided for my mother and the family they built together. Whether I realized it at the time or not, knowing my stepfather was there for my mother and sister, provided me the freedom of mind to move on and pursue my own dreams.

I learned a lot about relationships, both good and bad, from my mother. Of the many relationship-related lessons my mother taught me, one of the most useful was the art of forgiveness. Relationships have been a challenging area for me because of the diminished personal control over the outcomes. I know how to navigate academic and career pursuits because, generally speaking, individual efforts are directly correlated to the level of success you can achieve. Matters of the heart are much more complex. Sometimes, despite your best and most concerted efforts, there is nothing you can do to improve or develop a relationship. During my early heartbreaks my mother would help comfort me, but at the same time make sure I understood that you can never "make" anyone love you, or even like you. Relationships take effort, but must involve mutual interest and mutual effort.

I remember as a kid of about seven having a best friend who lived on my block, and we used to play together all the time and for a period of time we were inseparable. This was the first time I can ever remember feeling like I was the most important person in the world to another person, and that person was the most important to me. It was a great feeling . . . until a new friend came along. Jealousy, anger, insecurity, all the typical emotions coursed through my little body, and naturally the more these emotions grew, the more it drove a wedge between us. This just made the "new friend" seem more cool, fun, carefree, and let's face it, less effort, than the friendship with me.

Slowly but surely, my friend would "forget" to invite me over to play, or have various excuses why we weren't hanging out as much as we used to. Whatever positive emotions I had were gone and quickly replaced by rage and venom. I recall one hot summer night in particular, after popping over to my friend's house unannounced and "catching him" playing with his new friend, the new friend basically told me off, and my friend didn't defend me. He just let it happen, and seemed glad to see me go. I ran home and cried and cried and cried.

My mother asked me what happened, and I exclaimed how I hated my former friend.

My mother inquired, "Do you really HATE him? I know you are hurt and angry, but is it really hate?"

"YES, I HATE HIM!"

My mother took the time to process with me exactly how extreme "hate" was, and the price I would have to pay for choosing to hate someone. She explained that hate is a choice, and one that I can control.

She continued, "Is it really worth hating someone? If you choose to hate someone, you always have to remember you hate that person, and then when you see him you have to make the conscious effort to treat him differently, and that just seems like too much work. There have got to be better things you can use your brain for than to worry about remembering who you hate. In the end, hating someone really hurts you more than it hurts the other person."

I never forgot this lesson, and throughout my life no matter how angry anyone has ever made me, or how much anyone hurt me, intentionally or unintentionally, I always reminded myself that it is not worth the effort to hate that person, since the negative consequences of that choice will ultimately cause me more harm. My mother was no doormat, however. She is a firm believer in forgiveness, and letting go and moving forward, focusing on your own positive outcomes. But forgiving does not mean forgetting. Letting go and moving forward doesn't mean letting people continue to treat you badly or hurt you again and again. Take control and decide what level of future interactions you will or won't choose to have with that person, but maintain your own well-being.

I have watched my mother, time and time again, forgive others and move past things that other friends and relatives were not capable of doing, to their own detriment. My mother taught me by her words and deeds to take the high road and make the most of your own situation, without having to diminish or harm others. Once upon a time I saw this as a weakness in her, and so desperately wanted my mother to stand up for herself and just tell people off and cut them out of her life forever. In time, I learned the wisdom of her approach, and realized it wasn't a position of weakness at all, but a position of strength. Some people may have become "non-entities" in her life, but by circumstance, not hatred or vindictiveness. I came to see how forgiveness is not just a gift to the person you are forgiving, but a gift to yourself as well. It is a gift of freedom and peace.

As much as I learned how to be an optimist and forgive others from my mother's example, even more importantly I learned how to forgive myself. And believe me, at times that was really difficult to do! The perfectionist in me has always driven me to be better than everyone else, but not just "sufficiently" better, but the best that I can be, setting myself above and beyond everyone around me.

Of course I haven't always succeeded in these endeavors, and I've created a lot of stress for myself in the process of learning when good is good enough. Along the way, I've emotionally beaten myself up for my mistakes, particularly those that diminished my "perfect" image to those around me. My mother and immediate family were well aware of how far from perfect I really was, but they did a good job of keeping my secret and letting me save face with others.

A huge part of my struggle to overcome perfectionism was learning to internalize the Serenity Prayer. In my childhood I wasn't aware of the prayer per se, but I received the message frequently from my mother. As a child, I hated being left-handed. There are many legitimate reasons for this hatred, and all the rest of you "normal" people can't even begin to appreciate the challenges and discrimination that we south paws endure. What's with those special lefty scissors? I never learned to cut straight, and have suffered many calloused fingers in the process. I've burned myself more than once using those old-fashioned oven mitts that were only insulated on the one side. I've frequently splashed myself, and whatever was in my hands, reaching around with my left hand to operate a right-handed water fountain. I've had more class notes end up on my hand, arm, and sleeve than I care to remember. Not to mention all the smeared papers, barely legible to begin with.

In school, I couldn't wait to graduate from pencil to pen, hoping I'd no longer erase my notes and exams with my uncomfortably curved hand, but alas the joke was on me. At least pencil was easy to clean off when washing your hands for lunch. Pen was not nearly as forgiving. Using the erasable ink that became popular when I was in school was never an option for me, since my hand would remove the ink as quickly as I placed it upon the page. I feel like I lived most of my pre-PC life with perpetual ink stains running from my left pinky to just past my wrist. My penmanship is now completely illegible, and I'm not even sure why I attempt to even take notes in meetings. I guess so it will look like I'm really engaged for those around me. I try to input notes into my Blackberry as much as possible, but people assume I am being rude and checking email (yeah, I'm typically doing that, too).

I've cursed my left-handedness on numerous occasions, but my lamentations fell on deaf ears in my household. Both my mother and father are lefties, so no sympathy to be had there. If anything, my sister probably felt odd being the only righty. If I ever got a bit too whiney, my mother would be quick to put me in my place. "Is this something you can do anything about?" I don't think so. I could teach myself to be a righty, I guess, but basically it is what it is. "So, why would you waste your time and energy complaining and worrying about something beyond your control? Focus on what you can do and change."

In time I got over the shortcomings of being a lefty and celebrated the positive aspects of this natural inclination. Until that fateful day. I had previously mentioned my Jewish girlfriend (the one with the pregnancy scare) from high school. Her relatives were Reform Jews, and they invited me to join in their Passover celebration. I was very honored to be invited, and was on my best behavior. I understood the nuts and bolts of the Jewish holidays from frequent exposure growing up, and even knew a few Hebrew and Yiddish phrases. I felt adequately prepared, and was ready to act like a regular member of the family. The celebration ensued and we remembered why this night was different from all other nights; we then lit the candles; ate different foods in the prescribed order. All was flowing swimmingly, until one of the ritual moments when we were all to have a sip of wine. Oh the rueful lefty curse!

In formal settings I am typically pretty cognizant of my surroundings, proper place settings, and appropriate etiquette. Feeling comfortable and as though I were part of the family, I let my guard down and slipped from a more formal consciousness to natural instinct, and reached with my left hand for the wine glass. Normally this would be a minor faux pas, resulting in an awkward struggle for the glass or accidentally drinking from my neighbor's glass, but not this night. Oh no, this night was indeed different from all other nights.

It is customary at the Passover feast to provide a vacant place setting for the prophet Elijah, and leave the door accessible so the prophet may join you. As luck, or the lack thereof, would have it, the vacant place setting for Elijah was at the head of this Passover table. I was placed in the end seat on the one side of the table, immediately to the right of the vacant place set for Elijah. In my casual left-handed reach for what I believed was my wine glass, I inadvertently grabbed Elijah's cup, and then proceeded to drink from it.

While my girlfriend and her mother and brother chuckled a bit, her very elderly and traditionalist grandfather did not. He began yelling at me in some language I didn't understand, possibly something eastern European, though I distinctly believe I heard "Goyim" shouted, surrounded by angry guttural tones. The next thing I knew, her grandmother and the housekeeper are clearing the table as quickly as possible, throwing away the uneaten food and wrapping the dishes in some old looking cloth. Despite my perceived acumen in Judaism, I had no clue what was going on.

My girlfriend's mother swept me from the room, and instructed my girlfriend and her brother to take me upstairs and keep me there until things settled down. Once upstairs, my girlfriend explained that all the dishes and silverware were now going to have to be buried in the yard for a few days to cleanse them. Cleanse them? How does putting something in dirt make it clean? I was thoroughly confused. Why not just put everything in the dishwasher. They even had a kosher kitchen with two dishwashers and different cabinets for the different dishes so the dairy items would never interact with the meat items.

Evidently, the grandfather was not aware that I was not Jewish, and after my blasphemous debacle with Elijah's cup, either it hit him or someone said something to him in his native language explaining away my foolishness, and he felt I contaminated the entire feast and everything involved with it. Everything had to be returned to the earth, and in doing so, would restore the balance of the universe within this home and family.

Her mother finally came upstairs after what seemed an eternity, and suggested it was best that I go home. Her father drove me home, and initially we just sat in silence. He was a very large, intimidating man, and I kept having images of Tevye from *Fiddler on the Roof*. I finally garnered the nerve to speak. "I . . . I . . . I'm really sorry. I didn't know . . . it was an accident." I could see his face start to scrunch up, in what I initially thought was preemptive to a fit of rage. Much to my relief, he burst out laughing. His laughter continued to the point of being uncomfortable. He finally stopped laughing, and just shook his head and said it would all be OK, but I probably wouldn't be invited over again for any High Holy Days. I could live with that, but I felt such remorse. It really was just an accident, but I embarrassed myself, ruined their holiday, and caused a spiritual chasm for the grandfather. Not to mention all the effort that would be involved in burying, retrieving, and cleaning all those dishes.

When I got home and relived the horror for my mother, she assured me that the family had likely already forgiven me (OK, maybe not the grandfather), and now it was time to forgive myself. Regardless of what we say or do to others, and how they choose to respond or not, ultimately we can only control our own reactions and responses. In a world where we are surrounded by guilt, no wonder it is so difficult to forgive ourselves, even after other people have bestowed their forgiveness upon us. The Catholic and Jewish traditions are steeped in guilt, among others, and from the time we are children we are bombarded with messages that are intended to make us feel badly about ourselves, hoping to control and manipulate our behavior to some socially (or personally) accepted and desired end. Even religious messages of forgiveness are guilt-laden. At the same time we are intended to celebrate the ultimate sacrifices paid to remove our sins, the message is often manipulated by the human messengers to instantiate the guilt we should feel for that sacrifice, and subsequent burden associated with earning the privilege of forgiveness. It is a rather counterintuitive notion to have unconditional love and forgiveness, but have to feel forever sorry for what you did wrong to make it necessary in the first place (euphemistically of course, since I don't recall physically being present to either bite nor encourage the biting of any apple).

Psychosocially it makes a lot of sense why we struggle with forgiveness, particularly with forgiving ourselves. Some parents, and then later loved ones, feed the paranoia, doing irreparable harm. That is a shame. I feel incredibly blessed to have a mother with enough common sense and balance of purpose to have helped guide me through the mixed messages that bombard us from birth. Truly none of us has a time machine and despite our desire, as so eloquently expressed by Cher to "turn back time," that is simply not an option.

You can reflect on the past, but you must do so in terms of the realities of the present, with an eye toward the future. Helping me to learn how to rise above the dysfunction of guilt is one of the best gifts my mother has ever given me. That single gift has empowered me to remain focused on that which truly matters in life, remaining optimistic and desiring to improve both my personal circumstances and the circumstances of others.

This lesson is frequently applied in my professional life. Whether it is working with staff members, students or their parents, I constantly encounter people who allow themselves to be crippled with guilt and/or pessimism. What complicates matters is when people desire to shift responsibility thinking this will diminish their guilt, yet typically the opposite occurs. I believe most people have enough internal conscience and moral compass to know what they should do, but our litigious society continuously sends us the "accept no blame" message. Deny everything and hope the other side doesn't have enough evidence to convict you. Luckily college student conduct doesn't work the same way as a court of law and my focus is developmental not punitive. However, that doesn't keep students (and too often their parents) from taking approaches that are more indicative of television law shows than how anything actually functions in the real world. Often the real cause of these behaviors is the internalized guilt. Once we can get past that, then real growth and change can occur. Sadly, some can never get past it.

Despite what may come across at times in this book as pessimism toward our newest generations and shifting parental approaches, I truly am an eternal optimist, appropriately balanced with realism. Do I believe we have some difficult times ahead? Absolutely, but I see great heart among today's youth. Many are not equipped for the difficulties of modern life, and unfortunately daily crisis on college campuses is the new normal. However, I have great faith that many will rise above the challenges and prove to be great future leaders, if we let them. The biggest obstacle remains the strong desire to solve problems for them and shelter them from harm. We need to forgive ourselves and through that forgiveness set a new course toward a more optimistic future.

# CHAPTER 6

# TOUGH LOVE

Throughout this book I have tried my best to give you a glimpse into the window of my world and the manner in which this world has been shared and influenced by my mother. Many people, places, and events have influenced me, but my mother helped me learn how to control the level of impact I allowed those people, places, and events to have on my life. I've done my best to accurately and adequately portray this woman and her warmth, love, support, sacrifice, and mettle. In sharing the stories and vignettes of my past, hopefully you've recalled similar situations from your life and people who have taught you the same lessons I've learned. If you are a parent, maybe you've seen the same techniques you've employed in teaching your own children, or reflected on challenges you've experienced. My goal is in part to honor my mother, in part to provide a little comic relief, but more so to take pause and reflect on the outcomes of childrearing and our educational systems that are producing the young adults with whom I work daily, and express my concerns and hopes for their future.

The term "tough love" has been around a long time and is fairly self explanatory. Like so many of life's lessons, none of what I've discussed is rocket science. The basic principles of life are pretty simplistic, but the application can be very difficult. Just like the basic concepts of weight management or money management are known to all of us. Eat the same or fewer calories than you burn in a day and you will maintain or lose weight. Spend less than you earn and you will avoid debt and over time generate savings. These are simple concepts. So why do we live in a society of mass obesity and uncontrolled debt?

Simple principles are easier understood than practiced. I'm no exception. I come from a family of heavy people, and in my youth I struggled to make sure I would not become one of them. Somewhere along the way, life happened and I stopped exercising regularly and started eating more for speed and convenience than nutrition, oh yeah and got older, and now I weigh more than I desire. I practice most of what I preach. By American middle-age standards many might consider me "just right" and I've been told I look young and healthy for my age (and certainly for my level of professional stress). At the end of the day, I know what I look like out of my clothes and how I feel walking up and down a flight of stairs, and I'm not exactly where I'd like to be. This is again where my mother's wisdom provides some comfort. I can hear her in my head saying, "It's probably best that everything isn't perfect, because what would you have left to strive for? Besides, life's too short not to enjoy that cannoli, just don't eat the whole box."

One of the things I've enjoyed most about my mother, especially now that I'm an adult and am not on the receiving end of her tough love so much anymore, is her ability to give just the reality check that is needed when it is needed. For a brief period of time I was in a band. I was the lead vocalist, despite my lack of qualifications, particularly for the style of music we were trying to emulate. Our band was called "No Refund," which should paint some picture of the level of quality even we felt our band possessed. The bass guitarist was the founder of the band, and a good friend of mine. He would open each show, introducing us as "No Refund" and then quickly follow with the disclaimer, "so if you don't like us, F . . . . you, there's no refund!" We'd open with Lou Reed's "Vicious," then throw in a few original songs written by our fearless leader, and sprinkle in some Billy Joel (since I could actually hit most of the notes in the Billy Joel songs we selected, unlike our opening number). We represented an eclectic genre ranging from hard rock to punk rock to what is now called soft rock or pop, though at the time we would have been mortified to consider ourselves as such. Even our band members were incredibly diverse in our personalities, styles, appearances, and musical tastes. At the time I was more Duran Duran and Michael Jackson (with a splash of Broadway show tunes but we never talked about that), the drummer was more Flock of Seagulls and the Cure (though I think he too was a closet show tunes lover), the lead guitarist was more Beatles and Led Zeppelin, and our bass guitarist was our wild card, kind of all over the map, being the true music aficionado who could appreciate just about anything from classical to house. For purposes of the band, he seemed to favor more head banger and hair band style that was en vogue in the mid-80s. I never could quite pull that off, but I did my best.

This was all happening at a time in my life, between eighth and eleventh grades, when I was experimenting with my own sense of style and persona, and seeking to be the ever adaptable chameleon who could socially survive in any setting. Being an honors student and taking AP classes, I needed to compete academically and know how to work the preppy angle, and did that well with an alligator emblazoned upon my chest (where I went to school most of the really smart kids were preps, not geeks). I was also a choir geek, but needed to blend into the band geek world (two very different species of geeks) despite my lack of instrumental talent, for the sake of "No Refund." I had also forged a bond with the dirt bags, mostly for protection, and that required keeping a tattered denim or leather jacket stashed in the locker for quick application at lunch or after school for smoke breaks behind the cafeteria or gym. Since the dirt bags weren't in any of my classes, they didn't really know what I did with my time during the day, assuming I could never be smart enough to take academics seriously. There could be some overlap between the band geeks and dirt bags, and some overlap between the preppies and the choir geeks, but I tried my hardest to keep my various worlds separated. I even had a brief and somewhat successful foray in the world of the jocks, earning a varsity letter for Badminton and serving as the team manager for the girl's team (I was dating one of the first strings at the time). I also got involved with the theatre and dance crowd, which overlapped with the choir geeks a good bit, but the parties were much better.

I dabbled in just about every group that would allow me in, or at least made appearances in the ones who would let me slip through the cracks until they noticed my presence. I was building a resume for college after all, so I needed sufficient face time with student government, the Spanish club, the Yorker club, etc. I was never popular, but I had my own little fan club and they served as good buffers to represent me to the various groups when I was busy representing (or at times misrepresenting) with other groups. I also had a fully engaged world at church, being involved in the choir, youth group, service projects, retreats, Bible study, etc. Life was pretty busy, and there was much to juggle between school, co-curricular activities, church, dating, household chores, helping to care for my sister, and earning money however I could. I didn't sleep much, and when I did, I was a very vivid dreamer, and sometimes awoke far more exhausted then when I went to bed, so why bother. In retrospect, I'm amazed at the things we could accomplish in our youth.

One quick side note I'd like to share about busy lives. My mother is a firm believer, as am I, that generally speaking the busier we keep ourselves the less time we have to get into trouble, and the more we will accomplish by having sufficiently structured and scheduled lives. Though I still found a way to schedule in time for some trouble in my youth, I can only imagine the extreme level of destruction I would have unleashed on the world had I not been as busy as I was with other productive activities. In many ways I believe my busy life saved my life. I also enjoyed my greatest academic success during the semesters I took the most classes, worked the most, and was the most involved in college. But the life lesson I really want to acknowledge here is time management. I now teach classes and seminars on time management to college students, and I work with enough students at all stages of their academic careers to know how critically important good time management is to their academic, social, and future career success. Yet over the past twenty years I have found that students, while living much busier and structured lives prior to entering college, have significantly diminished time management skills. The reason, I believe: they are not managing their own lives, but having their lives managed for them, without anyone ever bridging the gap from "doing for them" to "teaching them" how to do things for themselves.

When I entered junior high school and made the shift from the elementary school model of spending the majority of the day in one room to then having to move from room to room roughly every forty-five minutes, my mother purchased a small calendar and day planner for me. She helped me take my class schedule and create a daily plan, then helped me extrapolate that to a weekly plan (certain classes didn't meet every day, so I had to learn to distinguish between a Monday schedule and a Thursday schedule), then fill in my other out of class responsibilities, and block time for homework, limited favorite TV shows, etc. Then as the term continued and we would get planning schedules from teachers with details about due dates for papers and exam dates, we would enter those details on the monthly planner. She made it clear that my calendar and planner was just like my house key, and should be with me at all times (while I wasn't familiar with the term at the time, I would have been considered a "latch key kid" since I had to secure the house on my way out and let myself in after school). From that point forward, for the rest of my life, I would have a calendar and planner of some kind. Hard copy initially, growing in size and complexity in correspondence to my life, then eventually transitioning to electronic formats that would sync with portable devices, evolving now to my addictive use of a Blackberry.

Once I was in junior high, my mother made it very clear that it was MY responsibility to keep up with my schedule and be where I needed to be and on time. She would periodically guide me in the process, but she also reiterated that she would not be my personal secretary nor my personal chauffer, and I needed to rely on myself to manage my time and transportation (which granted is easier to do growing up in an area with comprehensive public transportation). So when people ask me how I became such a great time manager, I give all the credit to my mother because she made me be a good time manager. When I messed up I suffered the consequences of missing activities I enjoyed or getting a diminished grade if I neglected to turn in an assignment on time, and the next time I did a better job of managing my schedule and responsibilities. Again, none of this is rocket science, but if you grow up with somebody always taking care of these things for you and making all of your decisions for you, how will you ever know how to do it for yourself?

Thank you for indulging this digression, and now back to the main story. Even being the very skilled chameleon that I was, changing both my persona and my look, often multiple times throughout the day, I had to pick a base look from which the various transformations would occur. This took thought and skill, contemplating what constants could be minimally acceptable across the spectrum. I had some successes and some abysmal failures, and my mother was right there every step of the way with her own brand of tough love and support. As I became more adventurous, the stakes got higher. Add an earring in your left ear. Start small, a diamond stud, now slap in a safety pin for smoke breaks with the dirt bags.

Wear the Izod pull over, but pull the collar up in class with hair down, then after school collar down with hair up, and cover the alligator with a denim jacket. You could traverse the continuum with some minor accessorizing when playing the role of chameleon. I was also a big Boy George and the Culture Club fan, and Karma Chameleon became my theme song. Despite the wide array of diverse tweaks I could make throughout the day to achieve my various looks and personas, I still had kept my core look pretty conservative. The challenge was my hair color.

As a young boy, I had beautiful golden blond hair, and it framed my face in a cherubic fashion that helped create the sweet and innocent image that masked my inner hellion. Had my hair been a different color growing up, I might not have gotten away with as much as I did, but who knows. As I grew older, my hair turned darker, into what I considered a very unattractive and bland brown. I grew up close to Jones Beach on the south shore of Long Island, and in the summers I would ride my bicycle down to the beach and spend a lot of time in the sun. Remnants of my former golden locks would emerge as the season progressed. To enhance this process, I started using hair lightening products like Sun In. The challenge would be the intermediary phase of sickly orange that first emerged until the blond finally arrived. My mother and grandmother both dyed their hair (at home, funds were tight), so I started paying close attention to the products they used and the processes involved. I then discovered what I believed to be my magic bullet: creme developer and peroxide. Quicker and more powerful than Sun In, I could strip the color out of my hair and get to blond, or even white, whenever I wanted, summer or winter.

Not ready to make the full transition, I started with just a test sample. At the time, "rat tails" were all the rage, and I too wore the long dangly thin strip of hair travelling down from the back of my head ending just between my shoulder blades. I proceeded to douse my rat tail in the stinky white gooey liquid, and then wrapped it in tin foil to keep it from running onto my neck and back, which I later learned the hard way can burn your skin pretty badly. After about twenty minutes and a quick rinse, there is was . . . my golden hair returned.

This background is important, because just like the warnings we received about smoking cigarettes leading to smoking marijuana, which would then become a gateway drug to more serious and dangerous drug use, dying your rat tail can have the same effect. Since the newly blond rat tail was received so positively in junior high, it seemed logical to take the next step and go completely blond. This, too, was initially well received, though my home hair care lacked the necessary consistency to generate the same shades of blond/white each time, making it difficult to convince people that "this just happens naturally."

This evoked one of the many steps in my mother's 12-step program of tough love. Don't try selling it if nobody's going to buy it.

"But Mom," I would plead, "if I do it right before school starts, I can say it came from the summer sun, then it just stuck around all fall, then we say we went somewhere sunny over Christmas break and that is how it is still blond in January."

Mom's classic response, "Just how stupid do you think people are? And how stupid does it make you for trying to lie? If you want to dye your hair blond, do it, and own it."

In retrospect I can't even imagine why back then I would have wanted to make people believe that my color transformation was natural. Like many kids during the difficult junior high/middle school years, I felt the need to exaggerate, misrepresent, and downright lie to impress the other kids and teachers at times. I'm sure I wasn't the only kid who periodically told a fib, and I imagine each one of us lived with the perpetual stress of being found out. Sure we all knew the same old shtick about lying being bad . . . blah, blah, blah. My mother's approach focused more on logic. She would explain, when you tell a lie, you need to remember the details of that lie, and be able to recreate the lie over and over. As you add more lies into the mix, the complexity of recreating an alternate reality becomes virtually impossible.

Even more impactful than her discussions of lying, were her perspectives on honesty, and the gray area between the two. There is outright lying, there is dishonesty by omission, but there are also shades of honesty ranging from blatant and sometimes hurtful honesty, and more tactful and selective approaches to honest communication. My mother always had a great rapport with young people, and was very active with teaching Sunday school and advising youth group. I credit her success with her ability to be honest in ways that other adults were often not willing or able to be. Some things in life are what they are, so why beat around the bush or unnecessarily sugar coat things? There is no need to be cruel, but being direct can create beneficial results, even if the recipient doesn't realize it yet.

This leads to another step in my mother's 12-step tough love program: Don't ask a question if you are not prepared for the answer. "Does this super tight bleached out t-shirt with patches stapled on it and ripped at the neck and arm look stupid on me?"

"Why, yes, it does. But if you like it, wear it."

This taught me both to consider carefully when asking for my mother's opinion if I was prepared for the response, but it also taught me to place the appropriate qualifiers on my responses when other's asked my opinion. Are you really doing your friends and loved one's any favors when you lie to them, even if you tell them a little white lie to make them feel better at the moment? What if they learn from another source brave enough to give a more honest response that your response was polite but dishonest?

There is shared and mutual responsibility between both parties in such forms of communication, so it is best to discuss the parameters first, then the topic at hand. Many people struggle with the embarrassment factor when confronting or communicating with others. Do I tell my co-worker she has a booger hanging out of her nose? Do I tell my boss his fly is down? It may not be my responsibility to have to tell them, but wouldn't I want someone to forewarn me and help me avoid potential embarrassment? If people don't appreciate the intrusion or find it inappropriate that I approached them to share my observations, it is really their issue, not mine.

So, let's get back to my hair. As expected, I grew bored with my bleached blond hair and wanted to spice things up a bit. I purchased what I thought was a wash-out temporary red hair dye. Evidently I didn't read the fine print, which explained that the wash out process was not guaranteed to work immediately, and when applied to hair that was already chemically treated, the results could include both a deviant color from the package and a delayed removal process. I suspected something went terribly awry as I was leaned over the side of the tub watching an odd shade of reddish purple run off into the drain. I proceeded to towel dry my hair, ruining a perfectly good towel with terrible stains, and then I looked in the mirror. The outcome was not at all what I expected or desired, but I held out the false hope that by morning and after an additional shampoo that the color would settle into the shade I had desired. All of this took place on a Saturday night.

Come the next morning, after my shower, the result was no better. Time was ticking and I couldn't avoid my mother much longer before we needed to leave for Sunday school and church. As I walked through the kitchen heading back from the bathroom returning to my bedroom to get dressed, I prayed that my mother would not turn around. I said "good morning," and quickened my step through the kitchen, rounding the corner to the stairs thinking I was home free when I heard, "get back here."

I paused, but knew I could avoid the confrontation no longer. I turned around and headed back into full view. "What did you do!" my mother exclaimed.

"Well, I had a little accident with some hair dye, but it will all wash out soon, it just takes a few shampoos. Since I don't look presentable for church, I guess I'll just stay home."

I'm not sure what made me think this would work, but as expected my mother's response was clear and direct. "I don't think so. You made yourself look this way, so deal with it."

Despite my mother's personal feelings about what I did, she went through the day at church completely unfazed. I wore a hat to diminish the impact, but it couldn't completely hide the damage. We both endured a variety of comments, laughing some off and tried to ignore others. However, there was one particularly judgmental and harsh member of our church, and he seemed to delight in criticizing my mother whenever possible. He didn't believe in divorce, so my mother already had one strike in his book, and he believed in the most restrictive approach to parenting his two daughters, both younger than I (both of whom became unwed mothers the minute they left his house—no judgment, just sharing the facts). He also felt my mother was far to open-minded and accepting to work with the youth group, and felt a hard line of abstinence in all things was the only acceptable approach when dealing with Christian youth (I enjoyed the irony of his daughters' conditions a bit too much when I heard).

My mother didn't necessarily disagree with the core values he espoused, but didn't agree with the restrictive and unrealistic approaches he attempted to dictate to the church leaders. The minute I saw him entering the church I knew there would be trouble. He approached me with a quickened and marked gait, questioning how I could even show my face in the church looking as I did, and so disrespectfully wearing a hat. He snatched the hat off my head, grabbed me tightly about my bicep and said, "If you were my kid I would have killed you by now."

Even if my mother shared his sentiments from time to time, it was not his place to intervene in this manner. Not being able to control my sharp tongue, I responded, flatly, "Well how Christianly of you."

This angered him greatly, and I really thought he was going to strike me. Luckily another gentleman, who was close friends with my mother, was standing nearby in the narthex and intervened, instructed me to move along. He shared the details of the encounter with my mother. After church, my mother asked me to take my sister and go wait in the car as she approached the confrontational church member. Naturally I didn't follow her instructions, but instead stood around the corner so I could hear what she had to say. My mother walked right up to him and said, "We need to talk."

He began to speak and she quickly cut him off, "I understand you grabbed my son earlier today. This is unacceptable. What my son does and how he looks is between me and him, and if you have concerns about my son you bring them directly to me. I don't care if you agree with me, but I would rather he be here, even looking foolish, than not attend church at all. Teenagers make mistakes, but kicking them out of church is not the answer. I hope we have an understanding."

Without letting him get a word in edgewise she turned and walked out of the church. As she passed the corner where I was standing, without even looking at me, she said through gritted teeth, "get your ass in the car."

We drove home in silence. I knew she didn't agree with what I did, and she disapproved of my disrespectful response, despite how reasonably provoked I may have felt. But, she wasn't about to let someone abuse her child, especially in church of all places, where people should feel safe and supported.

This wouldn't be her only encounter with this particular church member, or mine. Later that same year I had purchased a charm for my necklace that I really liked. For my confirmation, my mother bought me a beautiful gold cross with a small diamond in the middle. My grandmother bought me an Italian pink gold small link chain upon which to wear the cross. I wore the cross and chain daily. Months later, as I began dating more regularly, I became enamored with David Lee Roth's "I'm Just a Gigolo." As an outward symbol and embodiment of my desire to be a player, I purchased a playboy bunny charm, then I had a diamond soldered into the eye. I wore this charm on the same chain alongside my confirmation cross. This was just too much for that particular member of my church, resulting in another more heated confrontation between him and my mother. She again walked away victorious.

Do consider this story in context of the era. In the 1980's in New York, especially on Long Island, big hair, lots of gold jewelry, and outrageous clothing were very much the norm. My pseudo Guido adornments were not at all out of the ordinary, and playboy bunny paraphernalia was readily attainable in every flea market and corner store. Little playboy bunny mirrors, charms and other accouterments were given as favors at parties and Bar Mitzvahs. I may have crossed the line by adding a gaudy diamond-emblazoned gold playboy bunny charm immediately next to and resting upon a beautiful and tasteful cross, but in many ways this was indicative of the dichotomous developmental conflict I experienced at that time.

Let's also not forget that sometimes teenagers do things seeking attention, consciously or subconsciously, and I'm sure that was a contributing factor in my display. I typically didn't ask for my mother's opinions when making purchases or decisions about my external appearance because I knew she would tell me exactly what she thought, and that it would not be what I wanted to hear. So why bother to waste both of our time and leave us both unsatisfied. However, as I continued to push the boundaries further and further, the reactions I received from others grew more extreme. My mother was always there to defend my right to make my own choices, and she genuinely believed it. She didn't like it, and she would have preferred that I not make some of the choices I made, but that wasn't as important to her as protecting my right to make those choices.

I'm pretty sure my mother never read any Voltaire, or would think to attribute her beliefs on freedom of thought and expression as underlying democratic values to Voltaire, but I believe they would be on the same page. It didn't matter if my mother agreed or disagreed with what you thought, said or did, she would defend your inherent right to think, say, or do as you believe to be right for you (assuming of course there was no violation of other critical ethical principles, such as causing no harm to others, and seeking equitable and just treatment). However, my mother defended both sides of the sword of freedom. She always defended my right to be the individual I chose to be, but she also defended the rights of others to hold and express their viewpoints about my choices.

As I became more involved with the band and performing, my desire to experiment with more extreme hairstyles and colors grew. (It took me a while to get back around to this, but gentle reader, have faith that I always return to my points.) Despite the disaster of my experiment with red hair, and the subsequent months of effort that ensued to get my chemically fried hair back to a healthy enough state to begin the process of getting back to blond, I was ready to spice it up again. Bold colors, like neon blue, green, and orange, were all the rage. I had learned enough of a lesson to research my hair products more thoroughly before putting chemicals on my head, and found a temporary hair application that would tip the hair with a colored gel, hardening the sections of hair where applied, without chemically altering the hair color itself. It was the perfect compromise, and allowed me to enter the era of punk rock with a look that would be respectable for the audience and could be easily removed before school the next day. I also experimented with the wet look and thick, rigid applications of Tenax hair gel. Throughout my various iterations and significant variations of the "cool rocker look," I had my moments of weakness when the gibes of others would really get to me. I did my best to internalize my pain, but there were times I would turn to my mother for comfort.

True to her tough love approach, my mother would provide sufficient comfort to get me thinking rationally, then hit me with a dose of reality. I'll never forgot one of our most vivid conversations when I was feeling particularly wronged by the world and couldn't understand why people just couldn't leave each other alone and let everyone be who they wanted to be without judgment and hatred.

She retorted, "Wouldn't it be nice if the world worked that way, but it doesn't. People can be cruel, and there is nothing you can do about that sometimes. Yes, you have the right to be who you want to be, but some of the choices you make in doing so may have negative consequences. If you want to make yourself look like a freak, that is your right. But, if others want to look at you like you are a freak, or even call you a freak, that is their right, too. You can't get mad about it, just accept it, and then decide what you are willing to endure. It's not a matter of right and wrong, it's just a matter of reality."

This isn't necessarily what you want to hear from your mother, but it's what you need to hear. If you apply for a job that requires much interaction with the public, there will typically be an expectation that you dress a certain way and maintain a certain look. Life is about choices. If you want a certain type of job and you must look a certain way or behave a certain way to successfully acquire that job, then you must choose to do those things. If you choose to look or behave a certain way, and are unwilling to make any alterations for the sake of a job, or relationship, then you may only be able to find jobs or relationships that will accept the manner in which you are choosing to look and act.

Do not interpret this in any way to be a discouragement of diversity. My mother worked in a very diverse corporate environment, and both encouraged us and intentionally created opportunities for us to engage diversity of thought, lifestyle, religion, etc. My mother also encouraged us to confront that which we believed was wrong and create change wherever possible. She advocated first understanding the environment, circumstances, and appropriate channels of change before jumping into a situation half cocked and potentially making matters worse. Her approach to a reality based tough love was more about preparing us for the struggles we may encounter more so than encouraging us to accept the status quo. Your initial choices either get your foot in the door or not, then you make subsequent choices from there. In her opinion, the best way to engage change was from the inside, so making the necessary choices to get your foot in the door was generally a more advisable approach rather than a revolutionary kick-in-the-door approach. In my own experiences, I, too, have found that approach successful.

Like most things in my mother's life, she didn't just talk a good game, but she practiced what she preached. In my life I have embraced diversity in my choices of friends and dating relationships, and my mother has never blinked. Over the years I've brought home people who were Jewish, Catholic, Hindu, Mormon, white, black, Asian, Indian, blind, gay, bisexual, homeless, older, younger, international, rich, poor, every political and philosophical persuasion, and I imagine more variables of diversity that are failing to come to mind at the moment. Even when I entered into some serious dating relationships with people who my mother would not have chosen for me or honestly preferred I not date, she didn't intervene. She would express her honest opinion that some relationships, simply by the nature of the differences between the partners, would likely result in more difficulty than relationships that might be more homogeneous. This was never meant as a judgment, but more a precaution to allow appropriate reflective thought and preparation for managing potential hardships.

From my own experiences I have found my mother to be right. If I were to chose to marry a white, Methodist, woman of similar educational level, financial means, political viewpoint, and life philosophy, might we avoid certain conflicts that could arise if we did not share so many characteristics in common? Of course. But what happens when you fall in love with someone outside the pretty postcard? You live, you learn, you grow, you argue, and in the end, your life is likely richer as a result of the struggles, but enter those struggles with eyes open, expecting difficulties and perhaps discrimination. That was really my mother's bottom line. She wanted to shelter us from pain whenever possible, and prepare us to handle pain at times when she couldn't.

# CHAPTER 7

# REFLECTIONS

"The greatest gifts you can give your children are the roots of
responsibility and the wings of independence."
Denis Waitley

This last chapter, while drawing upon the themes of the previous
six, will deviate in structure and tone a bit. I've shared some critical life
lessons that I primarily attribute to my mother. Hopefully the stories
illustrated a few examples of each lesson, and provided some insight
and humor. This chapter is more about ways I've tried to apply what
I have learned and examples from my professional life of where it
seems some of these important lessons may not be as readily apparent
today. At the risk of sounding like a curmudgeonly old man giving an
armchair lecture that commences with "in my day . . . ," I beg for a
moment of latitude to share a few examples that are indicative of why
it seems some of these life lessons are not as engrained in the fiber of
subsequent generations.

In my academic and professional life, I've studied many theories
and philosophies of life, education, religion, culture, society, and
student development. As I mentioned in the Preface of this book,
I've long been a fan of Kohlberg's concept of growth resulting from
conflict. Even more influential in my mind and work, and more
direct and applicable, is Nevitt Sanford's theory of Challenge and
Support. In a nutshell, this theory espouses that growth results from
a continuous engagement and balance of challenge and support. At
the risk of over-generalizing the characteristics of entire generations
and essentializing all the members therein, it appears that Generation

X received more challenge with less support, and the Millennial generation received more support with less challenge (or at least independence of challenge). I'll also acknowledge that there is vast diversity within the myriad subcultures of American society, impacted by variables that I cannot begin to fully explore and for every statement I make here there is certainly an exception. My reflections are based on my lived experiences within my relatively vast or limited scope, depending on your perspective.

Many members of the generation within which I am labeled, at least for those of us born in the earlier half, were more likely in our childhood to be sent out to play, finding our own friends and activities to occupy our time, to be entrusted with house keys, and to be left alone to care for ourselves and/or siblings at fairly young ages. We got involved in little leagues, recitals, etc., but it was more likely that parents would not be present at regular practices, and many parents wouldn't have time to attend the games. At the end of the league, there were winners who got nice trophies, and the rest of us were losers. There were some "pity" awards, like most improved, best effort, or best attitude, but the majority of participants received nothing, other than the enjoyment and skill building from engaging in the activity itself. If life didn't naturally produce enough challenges for us, our parents may have created a few along the way, just to make sure we could handle these things should we ever have to.

The Millennial generation is much more likely to have friends chosen by their parents, scheduled through formal play dates, carefully monitored at all times by some adult supervision, engaging in activities chosen and coordinated for them, where everyone is a winner despite actual level of achievement, and with minimal risk of any real harm. These kids may be likely to have pretty purses and wallets with fake credit cards for play, but not likely to have a key hanging around their neck or any real money with which they need to make their own purchases. This generation has had the best, safest, most luxurious cradles, strollers, playpens, car seats, helmets, and toys.

I remember riding in the car as a kid without a seatbelt plenty of times, or strapped in to a lap only seatbelt, which I may have shared with other children at the same time. I never wore a helmet while roller skating or riding a bicycle, and we wouldn't have even thought to do so. This doesn't mean that these safety precautions aren't wise improvements, but the pendulum appears to have swung from minimal care to extreme care, possibly to a level of care that might have unintended negative consequences. When I have these discussions with friends I frequently receive the retort about how different things are today than when we were kids and how much more dangerous the world is. Actually, if crime statistics reports are accurate, by many measures our society has grown safer than it was in the 1960's and 1970's. There is certainly more media attention and sensationalizing and quicker transmission through the internet and social media, but do the facts support the perceptions we have been sold?

As a kid, we lived by the five second rule. If something hits the ground and you could get it up and in your mouth in under five seconds, it was "safe." Kids in the Millennial generation had bottles, nipples, and toy parts that could be sterilized to be as clean as surgical instruments. Generally speaking, kids from previous generations were exposed to unconditioned and unfiltered air, unfiltered water, germs of every kind, with basic soap and water solutions. Again, I'm not suggesting that our technological and lifestyle advancements haven't improved our lives and certainly we've been provided much higher levels of comfort, but we may have over-sanitized a generation, and then added significant levels of medication to control their every possible concern, and the full results of these choices may not be known for many years to come.

I am optimistic. Not just because it is my nature, but also because I believe the economic difficulties we are experiencing are creating a positive side effect. Parents may not have the means to satisfy their children's every desire anymore, and parents and their children may have to learn to make tough choices. The signs are already emerging from the post-Millennial generation that they are less materialistic, more fiscally conservative, and learning how to do things for themselves much more than the previous generation. I'm hearing from some of my friends with young kids that they are moving away from participation awards, and while they are still encouraging positive self-esteem, it is not being developed at the cost of skill development and quality assurance.

Younger kids, it seems, are learning how to lose and fail, and realizing it is OK, even good sometimes, and the experience of loss can generate learning and improvements for the future when they have to experience that first break up or a really bad grade. Nothing is sadder for me than a college student who feels compelled to take his or her own life because of a failing grade, getting dumped, or being bullied. I can't help but wonder if there were things that could have been done differently to help that student be better prepared for life's difficulties.

I still have five to ten years of Millennial students entering college to teach before the first classes of the next generation will grace my door steps, but I'm already seeing some good signs of change. From when I started my career about twenty years ago, I sensed a diminishing of skills and abilities each year as I engaged a new freshman college class, and I still don't think most college freshmen are where they need to be academically or socially, but the past few years each entering freshman class has been improving. They have overall still been far too coddled, and are attached to their parents in ways that may be unhealthy for independent adulthood.

Of course, I'm making a big assumption here. I operate under the belief that a primary goal of a college education, at least for traditional aged students, is to prepare them to succeed as independent adults, actively engaged in their professions and society. I consider it a personal goal to do everything in my power to help students leave college with clear plans for their future. Hopefully, that means not moving right back in with their parents upon graduation. That may be necessary for some for a period of time, especially in difficult economic times, but hopefully is not the norm.

Most parents I meet agree with me, at least publicly. However I also speak with far too many parents privately who have come to define themselves primarily through their children, and want college to become 13th through 16th grades, with little change in social or interpersonal dynamic. This isn't healthy for the student or the parent. Maybe some parents are vicariously living through their children, seeking experiences for their children that they themselves did not enjoy, but at some point it is still important that the parent sufficiently disconnect.

A case in point: I received a call from a frantic mother one afternoon. Her daughter was in my class, which had ended at 3:15 pm. She called my office at 3:45 pm. She wanted to know if her daughter was in class. Because of federal confidentiality laws and institutional policy, I wasn't allowed to provide that information without the student's permission. I inquired about the reason for the call (we are in college after all and we operate differently from high school). The mother explained that her daughter called her every Monday and Wednesday exactly at 3:15 pm as she exited my class, and the daughter didn't call that day. The mother called her daughter's cell phone, but she didn't answer. I offered a variety of reasonable explanations. Maybe she is meeting with classmates to discuss a class project, maybe she stopped off for coffee, maybe she entered a building with limited cell service (or maybe she just doesn't want to talk to you, though I refrained from sharing that thought). The mother grew hysterical and started wailing that she just knew her daughter was dead, and she was too far away to drive to campus to look for her and wanted me to go find her. Per our policy, I encouraged her to share her concerns with the campus police if she felt she had legitimate reasons to believe her daughter was in danger, but I did my best to calm her down and help her see that her fears were likely unfounded. There was nothing I could say to that mother at that moment to dissuade her from the belief that her daughter was in grave danger. Unfortunately, this is not an isolated incident and this is not the only parent who has placed such a call.

When I next saw her daughter in class, I asked her about it. The daughter was highly embarrassed and pretty upset at her mother for calling me. I encouraged her to discuss her feelings with her mother, and work together to set reasonable expectations of communication, but the daughter said, "I don't want to upset my mother. It is easier to just remember to call her after every class so she won't worry."

Fast forward a few years: if you were this young woman's employer, would you tolerate her having to call her mother after every meeting?

How would the employer respond if her mother called the boss to see if she had come to work that day? This may sound farfetched, but I'm hearing these stories from employers more and more (and experienced a few examples myself with some younger staff members). Parents are calling in for their students when they are sick and can't come to work, they are calling to negotiate employment offers, they are making decisions on benefits packages, and the list goes on and on.

There is nothing wrong with young adults seeking their parents' advice and guidance, and the parents can pass along their wisdom, but that is often not what is happening. Parents are making the decisions and directly managing all of the communication because they perceive they are better equipped to do so. Maybe that is true, but how will these young adults ever learn to do it for themselves? Each generation has great knowledge, skills, and abilities to transmit to the next, but the key here is the transmission not just the transaction. Stop giving the fish—take them fishing. Yes, it takes longer and may not yield the exact desired outcome, but it also creates an experience upon which everyone can reflect later in life, and sometimes the outcome actually exceeds the expectations. Everyone also needs good fodder for family reunions!

I speak to the parents of incoming college students at new student orientations, and share these thoughts, hoping the parents will heed my advice and empower their students to manage their own challenges and learn and grow, collaborating with me to create strong, successful, independent adults. Yet, the first week of school every fall, I learn of a parent (usually a mother) "hiding out" in her daughter's room. From the minute students move in, I start receiving requests from parents for a variety of things. I always ask for the student, and looking him or her in the eyes, provide a response to the request, and indicate that all future requests should come directly from the student. Sometimes this appears to anger the parents, which is not my goal, but is an unfortunate side effect of teaching their students to speak for themselves and begin their lives as independent adults (albeit in transition).

When parents call to report to me all the things going wrong in the student's room or class, most frequently involving roommate conflicts or mean professors, I ask to speak with the student. I regularly hear, "oh my daughter doesn't know I'm calling. I want this phone call kept confidential, but I want you to kick my daughter's roommate out because she let's boys spend the night, or change my daughter's class."

Legally I can't do these things, nor should I do them ethically. However, I am always willing to investigate every report I receive, and more often than not the details are highly inaccurate. Ironically, many of the complaints I receive from parents, upon investigation, end up being the opposite of what they believe, or minimally involve some code violation perpetrated by their own student.

I received a very angry call from a parent threatening to sue the university because his son was living with a drug dealer and he claimed his son reported it to us and we were doing nothing about it. Upon investigation, there was no report from the son, and it was actually his son who was found with excessive amounts of drugs and paraphernalia. When his son got arrested and kicked out of campus housing, the father called me back, again threatening to sue the university because we were too harsh on his son and had no right to invade his son's privacy. The father completely missed the point that it was his report that caused me to ask the authorities to investigate the claim. I have hundreds (maybe thousands) of these stories, so I'm not talking about isolated incidents of a rare unreasonable or over-involved parent. I'm talking about a pervasive social shift over the past two decades that causes me some concern.

I imagine at this point, some of you reading this feel I'm being a bit unfair on today's parents. It is reasonable to expect, especially in light of 17, 18, or 19 years of more involved and protective parenting than experienced in previous generations, that parents may have difficulty abruptly cutting all ties and expecting their "children" to all of a sudden behave like "adults." I completely agree. The transition from childhood to adulthood is a process, and it takes time.

Just as Lao Tzu said, the journey of a thousand miles begins with one step. That first step must be taken by the student. The parent can initially hold the student's hand, just as the parent did when the child was learning to walk, but at some point the parent let go, and the child walked alone. There may still have been a few stumbles, even some falls, but the child got up and continued walking, growing ever stronger. The transition to college is no different, except that there are many safety nets that institutions put in place to assist the process.

The transition process should be evolutionary over time. The first question that tells me a great deal about the roles played by the student and the parent is who completed the college application. The idea of my mother completing my college applications never entered my mind, and why would I ever think that it was her responsibility to do my work? Taking this one step further, who completed the campus housing applications? There is a reason why colleges want to know all that personal information about students, but we need honest answers provided by the students themselves to successfully do our jobs. I fully acknowledge that parents today, for the most part, do seem to know a lot more about their students personal preferences than in the past, but despite their beliefs to the contrary, they still don't know everything (and do you really want to?). My mother and I actually had a very open relationship, but we reached a point in life when she didn't really want to know certain details any longer, just as I would not have necessarily desired to know certain personal details of her life. Contrary to the self-inflicted transparency of Facebook, some privacy in life is still valuable and not everybody wants to know everyone else's business.

I do appreciate that parents' have some legitimate concerns and fears. They need a reasonable balance of knowledge to provide appropriate support. For example, when students call home feeling lonely, parents can let the student return home to familiar surroundings to resolve the loneliness, or encourage the student to get out and make new friends, and generate solutions to the loneliness that will propel the student forward toward independent adulthood. The first few weeks of college are so critical and parents may not realize they are interrupting a very normal stage of growth when they let students constantly come back home.

When students call home to complain about roommate conflicts, chances are the students are simply wanting to vent, and really aren't seeking any parental intervention. Parents can listen, commiserate, and maybe even question the student about what role he or she played in the conflict (it takes two to tango after all). Then parents can suggest ways the student can communicate with roommates to resolve the conflicts on their own, or guide the student to campus resources designed to assist in problem resolution. When the parents get involved in the conflicts, the situation is almost always worse for everyone involved. Parents have got to resist the urge to solve their students' problems and instead guide them to resolve and learn from their own conflicts.

For the record, I'm not just talking about freshmen or younger students. I get calls (sometimes threats) from parents with students who are 24, 28, 32, and even older. Nothing shocks me anymore, but I feel pity for these students . . . and their parents. Throughout my life I would periodically reflect on what my mother was doing in her life at that same age. Whenever I felt overwhelmed my last year in college, I would remind myself that my mother was working full time and caring for a husband and child when she was the same age I was at that point. When I turned 30, I reminded myself that at that same age my mother was already divorced with two kids, struggling to cover a mortgage, and working way too many hours in a newly earned management position, trying to compete in a good old boy corporate environment that was unforgiving and uncaring about personal family circumstances, especially those of a single mother. In comparison, I had it much easier at 30. When I receive some of these calls from parents of older students I have to pause and wonder how the caller would have reacted had his or her parent intervened in the same way back when the caller was at that same age?

Of course there are special situations involving students with disabilities or other legitimate circumstances that diminish certain capacities or require additional levels of care, but I'm not talking about those situations. There has been a substantial increase of older students returning to college, desiring a more traditional college experience, but also behaving like traditional students, complete with helicopter parents in tow. I felt my independence diminished at 16 years old when I was an early admission college freshman even asking my mother to sign certain financial aid documents because I wanted to do it on my own as much as possible. I could never have imagined her calling one of my professors to see if I was in class, or calling a campus housing administrator to discuss issues I was having with my roommate. My mother would have expected me to solve my own problems, with advice and guidance should I desire it. These are the parental values and approaches that helped establish my solid foundation for my future success.

I fully appreciate that parents cannot be blamed for the choices their children make, and even the best parental practices can yield delinquency beyond the parents' control. I've worked with some great parents who, like my mother, had kids who made some poor choices. However, I find it difficult to believe that a generation of young college freshmen who have been exhibiting some common behaviors and challenges just "became that way" when they arrived on my doorstep. Something has happened over the past eighteen years in their lives, and the behaviors I see their parents' exhibit didn't just develop overnight. There are many contributing factors, from schooling, to parenting, to peers, to external societal pressures, etc. There are no easy answers, nor do I propose some false Pollyanna images of superior Baby Boomer values that will solve all of our societal woes. The Baby Boomers did their own damage, and Gen X suffered some of the consequences.

Like I've said throughout this book, my mother wasn't perfect and I am not advancing her lessons as a universal model for parenting. I strongly believe she did something right, and I think there are lessons to be learned here, but those lessons must be individually vetted. Take what you will from this effort, and I do hope you gained something. Consider this less of a lecture, and more of a dialogue. If you have responses, reactions, praises, curses, emotional outbursts, or what have you, I'd love to hear it. Send me an email. I always respond to my email.

I'll close with one final message I frequently heard from my mother, particularly after her divorce from my father. She continually told my sister and me that in life we only had each other to rely on, and we needed to be there for each other no matter what. My mother came from a large family. Both of her parents had been married multiple times, and there were numerous sets of siblings from each of those unions. My mother generally played the role of Switzerland in her family battles, and witnessed the destructiveness of petty disagreements between relatives, particularly siblings. Since there was just the two of us, my mother wanted to make sure no matter what ever happened to either of us, the other would be there, forgiving any wrongdoings, and focusing on what really mattered.

As I got older and my father had additional children with his second wife, I did my best to develop healthy and supportive relationships with that family as well, but the bond between me and my sister was solidified by my mother in our childhood and will forever remain strong. I'm sure my mother feared, like all parents must, about what would happen to us if anything ever happened to her. It seems almost silly now in retrospect, especially considering I am closer in age to my parents than I am to my youngest half-sibling. My mother and I now joke about family discounts for elder care since we will likely spend more years of our life together in AARP than we did in my childhood.

I no longer believe that my sister and I only have each other in all the world to rely upon, though I know we'll always be there for each other. Our network of care is much larger and stronger, but every web has a center. Like the talented spider, my mother spun the web of support, but let my sister and I create the center, with sufficient strength that should the spider need to move on, the web would not just survive but thrive. We owe her much, and the best way I can repay the debt is to pay it forward, and hope you do as well.

# POSTSCRIPT

On March 19, 2009, my mother sent me and my sister an email. I haven't asked her permission to include it here, but I hope she won't mind too much. Attached to the email she included what initially appeared to be one of those annoying chain letters, but it was actually the poem "When You Thought I Wasn't Looking," by Mary Rita Schilke Korzan. I won't reproduce the poem here since it is readily available on the internet, but I will share what my mother wrote in her email. My mother had had a number of health challenges over the year prior to my writing this, and I had the pleasure of spending a few days with her during her recovery. When she was able, we talked about a variety of things, including stories from her youth and early adulthood, many of which I hadn't heard before. I'm not sure if it was the medication or the opportunity to have some uninterrupted time together without the distractions of holidays and relatives, but we really explored emotions to new depths. It was so rewarding to have the opportunity to interact in that way, but also made me appreciate how "precious and few are the moments we two can share."

Here is the email:

"Please read the attached. I hope that I may have shown you a few of these things "when I thought you weren't looking." I always tried my best and despite my failures, you both turned out to be wonderful, responsible adults! I am very proud of both of you and I love you both with all my heart (one of the parts I still have left!) Mom"

# ABOUT THE AUTHOR

Dr. Michael L. Sanseviro is the Dean of Student Success at Kennesaw State University in metro-Atlanta, Georgia. He grew up in Merrick, Long Island, NY, leaving at 16 years old to attend college at Emory University. Michael graduated Emory at 19 years old, completed his Master's at Florida State University at 21, and completed his Ph.D. at Georgia State University in 2006. Michael has over 20 years of experience working in higher education administration and teaches first-year college seminars and graduate courses. Having worked at numerous colleges and universities in multiple roles throughout his career, Michael has served thousands of students and their families, helping them successfully transition through the college experience.